Le Roy Clark Cooley

Natural Philosophy

For common and high schools

Le Roy Clark Cooley

Natural Philosophy
For common and high schools

ISBN/EAN: 9783744790352

Printed in Europe, USA, Canada, Australia, Japan

Cover: Foto ©Thomas Meinert / pixelio.de

More available books at **www.hansebooks.com**

NATURAL PHILOSOPHY

FOR

COMMON AND HIGH SCHOOLS.

BY

LE ROY C. COOLEY, Ph. D.,

PROFESSOR OF NATURAL SCIENCE IN THE NEW YORK STATE NORMAL SCHOOL.

NEW YORK:
SCRIBNER, ARMSTRONG & CO.,
SUCCESSORS TO
CHARLES SCRIBNER & CO.,
654 BROADWAY.
1872.

PREFACE.

THE great aim of this little book is to present the most elementary facts of Natural Philosophy, in such a way as to exercise the child constantly in observing phenomena and in drawing inferences from what he observes.

Whenever a child is old enough to ask such questions, as, " What makes the thunder," or, "Where does the rain come from," or to exclaim " How pretty the clouds are this evening," it is old enough to begin the study of natural philosophy. When such questions are asked the mind is awake to see the phenomena of nature, and is ready to receive instruction. They show the presence of a desire to know, and the absence of power to learn without assistance; and in this way they lead us to believe that the time has come when the work of instruction should begin.

Moreover, the study of natural philosophy is easy, and interesting to young pupils, because, when properly presented, it brings new sights to the eye, and new sounds the ear, in a way to be especially pleasant to children. The simplest experiments awaken enthusiasm in the mind of a child, and such as he may be able to repeat by himself are the source of the greatest delight.

This study is not only easy and interesting, it is also in the highest degree beneficial to the young, partly because of the valuable facts it imparts, but even more on account of the mental power it developes. The object of primary education should be to discipline the senses to habits of quick and accurate observation, and the mind to the habit of forming correct judgments from facts which the senses reveal. Natural Philosophy furnishes abundant materials of the most excellent kind, by means of which these objects may be accomplished. There are curious motions, beautiful colors and harmonious sounds, together with numerous other phenomena, which can be easily presented in the form of simple experiments, by which the skilful teacher can cultivate the power of the senses to furnish correct impressions, and at the same time develope the power of basing accurate judgments upon the impressions received. In a word, this study when properly presented is eminently fitted to teach even young pupils *how to gain knowledge for themselves* by observing events.

To this end, the following plan ought to prevail in presenting elementary facts. An easy experiment or some phenomenon of common occurrence, is to be introduced and the attention of the child directed to certain appearances and conditions, after which he may be called upon to notice the truth which these appearances suggest. A concise and accurate statement of the fact or principle itself, in form to be easily remembered, may finally complete the investigation.

Many of the experiments are such as pupils can make for themselves: let them be encouraged to do so; if they are, they will soon be bringing to the notice of the teacher, others which the text does not describe, and if the teacher will visit such efforts with marks of especial notice or reward he will soon find an enthusiasm in his class, which will make the pursuit of this study delightful and profitable to the end.

Another feature of this little book, which, it is believed, will commend it to the favor of both pupil and teacher, is the system of questions which runs through it. Every important topic in the discussion of each subject is introduced by a *question,* instead of by a *formal title,* as is customary. These questions will prove to be excellent guides, and really very important helps to the young pupil. The teacher will also find them serviceable in conducting the exercises of the class room, to which they are especially adapted, by being in immediate connection *with the text,* and in bold type *easily caught by the eye,* instead of at the bottom of the page or the back of the book, in fine print and compact lists. The eye catching them quickly, is not confined to the book; their use, therefore, will not be at the sacrifice of the vivacity and vigor of the exercise.

Albany, 1871.

NATURAL PHILOSOPHY.

PROPERTIES OF MATTER.

Describe the experiment with cochineal.—If, to try an easy experiment, we take a single grain weight of cochineal, and dissolve it in as much as a thimbleful of water, and then pour this small quantity into a gallon of clear water, the whole gallon will receive a beautiful crimson color.

Into how many pieces has the grain of cochineal been divided ?—Now a gallon of water is said to contain as many as 60,000 drops, and to color a single drop, all through, will take as many as 100 little particles of cochineal. If this is true, then the grain of cochineal must be divided into not less than *six millions of pieces !*

Can other bodies be divided ?—If an apple be cut into 100 pieces, each piece will of course be very small indeed, but yet it will not be so small that it can not be divided into pieces smaller yet.

The blow of a hammer may break a pane of glass into a thousand parts, but each one of these little pieces may by another blow be broken into pieces still smaller.

1*

What is divisibility ?—Every body of matter may be cut or broken into pieces. This is one of the qualities or properties of matter, and we call it *divisibility.*

Divisibility is the property of matter in virtue of which a body may be separated into parts.

Are examples of great divisibility common ? —There are bodies all around us so small that we can not see them. They are in the air we breathe and in the water we drink. Some of them are alive and some are not. Many of them are so very small that we need the most powerful microscope to see them at all. Yet every one is made up of pieces or parts which are of course smaller than itself.

For example: the dust which clings to one's finger when he holds a butterfly or a moth is made up of very small particles, and yet each of these little particles of dust, which we can scarcely see with the naked eye, is found, by using the microscope, to be made up of a thousand or more little balls.

Are living creatures so very small?—And then, too, there are living creatures so small, that it may need as many as a million of them to make a pile as large as a mustard-seed. Hosts of them are living in the air and in the water all around us. They are so very very small that it has been said that a thousand of them might swim or fly side by side through the eye of a needle.

And yet each of these little creatures must be made up of still smaller parts, or else they could not move about nor devour their food, as all of them are able to do. We can not even imagine how very small these parts must be.

What are molecules ?—If we keep on dividing a body into smaller and smaller pieces, we shall at last get to a piece so very small that it can not be divided again without changing it into some other kind of matter. These smallest pieces are called *molecules*.

Molecules are particles of matter which can not be divided without changing their nature. ▽

Does every body occupy space ?—Every little particle of dust, and even a molecule, must have some size. You can not even think of a body which should have no size at all. The very smallest body you can think of fills up a little room or space. And then every larger thing, a shot for example, or a cannon-ball; the world itself, so many millions of times larger than the ball ; and the sun, which is fourteen hundred thousand times larger than the world,—each of these bodies has its own particular size, or, in other words, each one fills a certain portion of space.

To occupy space is one of the properties of all matter : it is called *extension*.

Extension is the property of matter in virtue of which a body occupies a certain portion of space.

Can wood and water fill the same place at once? —If we fill a goblet with water, and then gently push a small stick down into it, the water runs over. We see in this way that wood and water can not be put into the same place at the same time.

Can water and air fill the same place at once? —Boys sometimes turn a goblet bottom upward, and then push it down into a vessel of water to see the air keep the water out of the goblet. The air will not let the water in, because they can not both be in the same place at once.

Can not a nail be driven into the same place with wood?—When a nail is driven into wood, the particles of the wood are squeezed nearer together so as to make room for the nail to enter. The wood and the nail do not fill the same space at the same time.

What is impenetrability?—No two bodies can ever be in exactly the same place at once. This is one of the properties of matter. It is called *impenetrability.*

Impenetrability is the property of matter which does not allow two bodies to occupy the same space at the same time.

Can not water and sugar be put into the same space at once?—Try an easy experiment in this way: fill a goblet to the very brim with water, so that not a drop more can be added without running over. Then take some fine sugar, and very slowly sprinkle it into the water. Quite a large quantity may be put into the goblet before a single drop of water will overflow. It would at first appear that water and sugar have been here put into the same space at the same time.

Describe the experiment with shot.—Take another goblet and fill it with shot, and then pour fine sand upon the shot. The sand will, of course, fall down between the shot, and a large quantity will be poured in before any will run over. Now the sand only fills up the *space between* the shot; no one would think of saying that the sand and shot fill the same space at once.

How does this explain the experiment with sugar and water?—Now the sugar and water act in the same way as the sand and shot. The fact is that water is made up of little balls or molecules, and the molecules of sugar are little enough to fall into the spaces between them. The two things do not occupy the same space at once.

What should we learn from the experiment?— We see that there must be spaces between the molecules of water into which the sugar falls. It is true also of all other bodies that there are spaces between their molecules. On this account bodies are said to be *porous*.

Porosity is the property of matter in virtue of which there are spaces between its molecules.

How was gold shown to be porous?—A long time ago, at Florence, a hollow globe of gold was filled with water, shut up perfectly tight, and then put under immense pressure. The water actually oozed through the gold, and, like a gentle dew, covered the outside. The water must have come through between the molecules of the gold, so that we know that even gold is porous.

What is elasticity?—We all know that a piece of india-rubber can be pulled out to a great length, and that it will afterward spring back again. We have also doubtless seen a steel wire straighten itself quickly after being bent. The quality or property which causes these bodies to spring back is called *elasticity.*

Elasticity is the property of matter in virtue of which a body springs back after having yielded to some force.

Is glass elastic?—The balls which boys use to play " marbles " with are sometimes made of glass, and every one knows how well one of these balls will bound upward when thrown upon the floor or pavement. Now the little ball is actually flattened at the moment when it strikes the floor, but the next instant the flattened part *springs* *back*, and it is this springing back which throws the ball into the air. This shows that glass is very elastic.

Are all bodies elastic ?—All bodies are more or less elastic. Lead and clay have but little elasticity, but even lead is elastic, for we find that two lead balls after being struck together will bound a little.

On the other hand, glass and ivory are among the most elastic solids we know of.

What becomes of water that boils away ?—When water boils, steam is formed. Now let us prove that all the water which disappears is changed into steam.

.We will first notice that when a cold body is held in a cloud of steam it is soon wet, which shows that by cooling the steam we get back water from which it was made.

Now let us put just *one pound* of water into a vessel and boil it. Let the steam pass through a pipe into another vessel which is kept cold. The steam goes over into the cold vessel, and is changed back into water. When the water is all "boiled away" from the first vessel we shall find just *one pound* of water in the other. All the water which disappeared was changed into steam. Not a particle was destroyed.

Is this true when the steam goes into the air ?—When the steam goes off into the air, as it usually does, its particles are so widely scattered that they disappear entirely, but every one of them is still in existence somewhere.

What becomes of wood when it burns ?—When wood is burned, one part of it is changed into ashes, and the rest changes into smoke and vapor. Not a single particle of it is ever destroyed.

What is indestructibility ?—Man may thus change

the shape and condition of bodies, but he can not destroy a single molecule of any thing. On this account matter is said to be *indestructible*.

Indestructibility is the property of matter in virtue of which it can not be destroyed.

What is compressibility?—When we squeeze a sponge in the hand we press its particles nearer and nearer together, and finally make the sponge much smaller than it was. Bodies which can be made smaller by pressure are said to be *compressible*.

Compressibility is the property of matter in virtue of which a body can be made smaller by pressure.

Is air compressible?—Air is very compressible. You may learn this from so humble a thing as a pop-gun. Before the stopper is blown out, the air behind it you can see to be crowded into perhaps not half the space it filled at first.

Is water compressible?—Water is very slightly compressible. Very great pressure is needed to compress it enough to show that it is compressible at all. A pressure which would compress air into less than a hundredth part of its natural bulk would not compress water, enough to be noticed.

Are all bodies compressible?—All bodies are more or less compressible. Air is one of the most compressible of all substances, and water is one which is among the least compressible.

Are molecules compressible?—All that pressure can do to a body is to push its molecules nearer together: we do not suppose that it makes the molecules themselves any smaller.

When air is compressed into a hundredth part of its

natural volume, its molecules have been pushed a hundred times nearer together than they were at first.

What is density?—Now when the air is so much compressed there is much more of it in a given space, a cubic inch for example, than there was before. In this condition it would be said to be more *dense*.

Density has reference to the quantity of matter in a given bulk.

What is inertia?—Masses of matter have no power to move themselves nor to stop themselves when once in motion. The clouds move along in the sky, not because they choose to do so, but because they are pushed along by the wind. An apple falls from the tree, because it is pulled down by an influence, soon to be described, called gravitation; and rocks rest in their places, not because they have any power in themselves to do so, but because they are held there by forces acting upon them. Bodies of matter have no power to change their own condition, and on this account they are said to be inert. *Inertia is the property of matter which does not allow a body to change its own condition of rest or motion.*

Are molecules ever at rest?—Masses of matter are often at rest; it is believed that molecules never are. On the contrary, it is thought that the molecules of every body are forever in motion.

You have perhaps seen a cluster of bees at the door of their hive, or of ants at the entrance to their nest, all huddled together and hurrying over and around each other in constant and curious motions. Now if our eyes were powerful enough to see the little molecules of which a block of wood is composed, it is thought that we should witness a scene of activity still more curious and constant, for every molecule in all the vast number which the block contains is in rapid motion. Philosophers believe that not a single one in all the world was ever for a moment still.

In what respect are the properties so far described, alike?—If we think again of the properties which we have just examined, we find that they are all of such a character that *a body may show that it has them without any change taking place in its nature.*

A smart blow with a hammer shatters a stone into fragments, and the experiment teaches us that the stone has the property of divisibility. But then every piece will be a piece of stone, and of just the same kind as before the blow; and so we find that a body may show the property of divisibility without any change in its nature.

What are physical properties?—All such properties,—that is, all properties which a body may show without any change in its nature,—are called physical properties.

What are chemical properties?—But all properties are not like these. Explosibility, for example, is one which a body can not show without a change in its nature.

Suppose a little gunpowder lies upon the table. You do not know whether it is explosive or not: it may be damp, and hence not explosive. But you touch it with a lighted match—a bright flash and a sudden puff occurs, and you say that the powder is explosive. Now all that is left upon the table at the spot is a dark stain. The powder itself has been changed into gases which have passed off and hidden in the air. No body of matter can show that it has the property of explosibility without changing to something else, and for this reason explosibil-

ity is called a chemical property. Chemical properties
are those which a body can not show without a change in
its nature.

What is natural philosophy?—Natural philosophy
is the science which treats of the physical properties of
matter and explains those things which occur without
any change in the nature of bodies.

The chemical properties of matter are to be described
in the science of chemistry: we need give no further
attention to them now.

ATTRACTION.

What is the effect of rubbing sealing-wax with flannel?—If we briskly rub a stick of sealing-wax with a piece of flannel or silk, we seem to give it a power which it did not have before, for if we hold it near to small bits

Fig. 1.

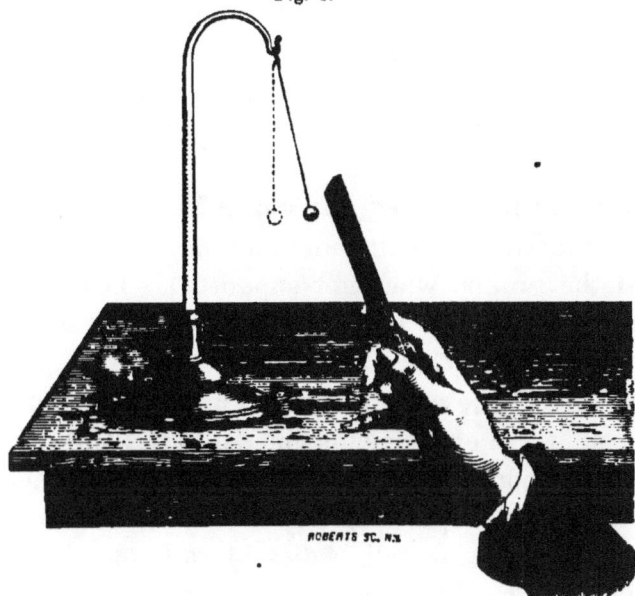

ROBERTS SC. N.Y.

of cotton we see them fly quickly toward it, or if we present it to a pith-ball hung by a silk thread, the ball will be drawn aside or lifted by it. (Fig. 1.)

What may be seen on the surface of quiet water?—If we observe the surface of quiet pools of water, we

notice that sticks and straws will not stay for any great
length of time upon the middle parts of the surface, but
that, instead of this, they will be gathered together around
the edges.

Or, if we wish to try an' experiment, we may put a
number of bits of wood here and there upon the surface of
water in a large pail or tub standing in a quiet place
where it may rest over night. In the morning we will
find the bits of wood huddled together, or against the side
of the vessel: not one of them staying alone where it was
placed.

What other facts of the same kind?—Other facts
of the same kind are still more familiar. A stone moves
toward the ground when not supported. Leaves fall to
the earth in autumn, and rain-drops and hail stones will
not abide in the sky.

What do these experiments and facts illustrate?
—Now all these experiments and facts illustrate the tendency of all bodies of matter to approach each other. If
they were not kept apart by some other forces this
tendency would cause all bodies to rush together. The
influence that would bring them together is called *attraction*.

Name varieties of attraction.—Attraction shows
itself in many ways, and when acting in different ways it
is called by different names. When magnets attract each
other the influence is called magnetic attraction. The
influence of the sealing-wax upon the pith-ball (Fig. 1) is
called electrical attraction. Besides these there are other
varieties, called cohesion, adhesion, and gravitation.

With the last three varieties we must now become
acquainted; but of the first two we shall learn more at
another time.

Why is a rod of iron so strong?—It is by no means easy to break a rod of iron. Every child knows this, but there are very few who can give a reason why the iron is so strong.

Just think of the rod being made up of molecules, as we have learned that all bodies are. These molecules would fall apart if there were not something to hold them together. They are held together by attraction, and the iron is strong just because this attraction is very strong.

How are the molecules of any body held together?—Just as there is attraction among the molecules of iron, so there is among the molecules of any other solid body an attraction which holds them together. This attraction acts continually. Were it to stop its action for the briefest moment, solid bodies would be seen instantly crumbling to pieces. Chairs, stoves, tables, and indeed the very walls of the house, would fall to powder finer and looser than ashes or flour.

The attraction which holds the molecules of a body together is called _cohesion._

Is the cohesion alike in all bodies?—Cohesion is much stronger in some bodies than in others. Iron is very cohesive but lead is not. It is easy to break a small rod of lead, while a rod of iron, of the same size, would resist all our power. It is because the cohesion is so strong in iron that this metal is so well adapted to use in making carriages, in building bridges, and in many other arts which you can easily mention, where great strength is needed.

If cohesion is strong enough to bind the molecules of a body firmly together, the body is a solid; but if it is very feeble indeed, the body is a liquid.

Are particles of different kinds of matter held together?—There is also an attraction between particles of different kinds of matter. When, for example, one writes upon the blackboard, he leaves fine particles of the crayon clinging to the surface of the board. Particles of water cling to the hand that is withdrawn from a bath in water; and it may be that particles of soil, clinging to the hand unpleasantly, made the bath necessary in the first place.

In all such cases we notice that there is an attraction between particles of different kinds of matter. Attraction between particles of unlike kinds is called *adhesion*.

By what experiment may we illustrate it?—A very pretty experiment is shown in Fig. 2. It illustrates the adhesion between water and brass. A round plate of brass, having a handle fastened to its center, is laid flat upon the surface of water, and then slowly and gently lifted. The water under it is also lifted a little, as the picture shows it.

Fig. 2.

You can use a plate of wood or of glass in the same way.

In what curious way may the adhesion between solids and liquids be shown?—If you will take two pieces of glass and put them side by side no farther apart than the thickness of a sheet of paper, and will then bring their lower edges carefully in contact with the surface of some colored water, you will see that fluid suddenly spring up an inch or two between the plates and remain standing at that height. In fact, it will stay up between the plates even if you lift them quite away from the water. It must be the attraction between the water and the glass which lifts the fluid and holds it up between the plates.

What is the effect when the plates are not parallel?—Still more curious is the effect if you will put the plates so that their edges will be nearer together at one side than at the other. The water jumps up as before, but its upper edge, instead of being horizontal as it was in the other experiment, will be in the form of a beautiful curve. The liquid rises highest where the plates are nearest together.

Suppose small tubes be used instead of plates.—When small glass tubes are used instead of plates, the fluid will rise still higher—just twice as high as between plates whose distance apart is equal to the diameter of the tube used.

It has also been proved that the liquid will rise highest in the smallest tube. It will rise *two* times as high in a tube whose diameter is only *one half* as great as that of another.

What is the law?—The law is this: the height to which the fluid rises is inversely as the "diameters of the different tubes." If, for example, one tube is *three* times the diameter of another, water will rise in it only *one third* as high.

What other examples of this action?—Water soaks upward through porous soils, and by this means they are kept moist and fertile. The oil is lifted through the lamp-wick to supply the flame above. Ink spreads through blotting-paper when only one corner of it touches the drop. All these and many other familiar things that might be named, are caused by the same influence which lifts water in small tubes or between glass plates. It is an attraction between solid and liquid bodies.

This attraction between solid and liquid bodies is very generally called capillary attraction, but it is really nothing different from adhesion.

Give examples of the action of gravitation.—A stone dropped from the hand falls swiftly to the ground, because there is an attraction between the earth and the stone. An apple bends its stem because the same kind of attraction is pulling it toward the earth, and when the fruit ripens and the stem has grown weaker, the same force causes the apple to break away and fall. This attraction is called *gravitation*. It is the attraction which acts upon all bodies and through all distances.

Give examples of pressure caused by gravitation.—Gravitation not only causes a body to fall if left without support, it also causes one body to press upon another on which it rests. A stone press s heavily upon the ground because gravitation is pulling it downward. All things upon the earth are held there, and exert their pressure, because gravitation is acting upon them. Some are held with much more force than others, as we may easily learn by trying to lift them. A pail of water hangs heavily upon the arm because gravitation is pulling it down.

What is weight?—It is easier to lift a block of wood than a stone of the same size, because gravitation is pulling the stone down with more power. To say that the stone is heavier than the wood means just the same as to say that the attraction of the earth upon the stone is stronger than upon the wood. Indeed, the *weight* of a body is only the measure of the attraction which the earth exerts upon it.

How do we tell whether two bodies have equal

weights?—A pair of scales enable us to tell whether bodies have equal weights. If we put one body in each scale-pan and the two are balanced, we know that gravitation is pulling one down just as much as the other; in other words, the two bodies are equal in weight.

What are sets of weights?—A piece of metal upon which the earth exerts a certain amount of attraction may be called an ounce *weight;* then another upon which the attraction is twice as great is called a two-ounce weight; and if upon a third the attraction is sixteen times as great as upon the first, it would be a sixteen-ounce weight, or a pound avoirdupois. Several such pieces of metal, made with care to represent the various units of weight, form what is called a "set of weights," to be used in weighing the various articles in trade.

In what direction does the earth attract bodies? — The earth attracts all bodies toward its center. From whatever point a ball is dropped, it will fall in a straight line toward the center of the earth.

This direction is always perpendicular to the surface of still water. You can easily examine this fact yourself by fastening a string to some heavy body and then holding or hanging it over a vessel of water, as you see it in the picture. (Fig. 3, p. 26.) The string shows the direction of the force of gravity * exactly, and it is easy to see that it is perpendicular to the surface of the water.

Such a cord and ball is called a *plumb-line:* builders use it to find out whether their walls are vertical.

Does gravity always cause motion downward? —While the earth's attraction is forever downward, yet it does sometimes produce motion upward. For ex-

---

* The earth's attraction is sometimes called gravity.

2

Fig. 8.

ample, it lifts the higher scale-pan of a balance by pulling the other downward at the same time, with greater force.

In the same way gravitation causes the upward motion of smoke by pulling the heavier air down under it, thus pushing it upward.

Why does a cork rise in water?—One more illustration will be enough. A cork at the bottom of a vessel of water quickly rises to the surface. Now it does not rise because it is light, as many people will say it does. The fact is that gravitation pulls both the cork and the water downward, but it pulls the water with the greatest force. The water must go down under the cork, and in doing so must push the cork upward.

Is the earth attracted by small bodies?—To say that the earth attracts an apple is not more true than to say that the apple attracts the earth. The truth is simply that they attract each other. The earth attracts every body great and small, and every one attracts the earth in return. Every leaf and every rain-drop or snow-flake that falls to the ground attracts the earth just as truly as it is attracted by it.

Is the earth moved by this attraction?—The earth attracting the rain-drop, makes it fall toward the ground; the rain-drop attracts the earth in return: can we suppose that the great earth moves up to meet it? We have seen thousands of rain-drops fall, but who ever saw the earth go up to meet them! And yet perhaps it does, for we could not see it if it did. The attraction would make the drops go as many times farther than it would the earth, as the earth is times heavier than the drops, and it would not be possible to see the motion through so small a distance.

Is gravitation confined to the earth?—But this force is not confined to the earth and the bodies near its surface: the sun and all the other bodies in the heavens attract each other. It is exerted by every body of matter upon every other in the universe. Grains of sand are held by it in their places on the sea-shore, and it keeps the sea itself from rising out of its bed. It is at the same time acting upon the earth itself and upon all the other heavenly bodies to keep them in their orbits.

On what does the strength of this force de-

pend?—The strength of gravitation depends upon two things: first, upon the quantity of matter in the body exerting it; and second, upon the distance through which it acts.

If the quantity of matter is doubled the attraction will be doubled also. Or, in general terms, *the attraction is in proportion to the quantity of matter exerting it.*

But if the distance be doubled the attraction will be only one fourth as strong. At three times the distance the force is only one ninth as strong. In general terms we say, *the attraction is inversely as the square of the distance between the bodies.*

What is the center of gravity of a body?—Boys are sometimes very fond of balancing books or ball-clubs, or even long poles, upon the end of a finger. They often become very skillful in doing this, without knowing that every time they do it they are trying an experiment in natural philosophy. The fact which the experiment illustrates is this: there is *a point in every body which if supported the whole body will be at rest.* This point is called the center of gravity. The ball-club has a center of gravity, and if the finger can be kept exactly under that point the club will not fall.

Illustrate by using a ruler.—Or, to study this subject further, let a ruler be balanced across your finger. There will be just as much of the weight of the ruler on one side of the finger as on the other, and a point exactly over the finger and in the middle of the ruler is the center of the weight of the ruler, or, as we have already named it, the center of gravity.

Every body has a center of gravity, and when this point is supported the whole body will be at rest.

Where is the center of gravity of a body?—The

center of gravity is not always in the center of the body. Suppose one end of your ruler to be loaded with lead : you would then have to put your finger nearer to the heavier end in order to balance it ; the center of gravity would be nearer to the loaded end.

When two boys are playing at seesaw the support of the board must be under the center of gravity, but if the boys are not of the same weight the support, as every one knows, must be nearer to the heaviest boy. The center of gravity of the board and boys together is nearer to the end where the large boy sits.

In Fig. 4 the center of gravity in each body is at G.

Fig. 4.

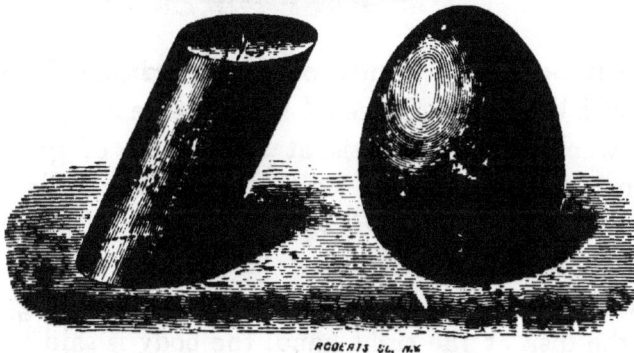

ROBERTS SL. N.Y.

What is the line of direction?—Now imagine a vertical line drawn through the center of gravity, as shown by the vertical dotted lines in Fig. 4. This line will show the direction in which the body would fall if it were left without support, and it is called the *line of direction*.

Where may we place the support for the center of gravity?—We may support the center of gravity by placing the support at any point in the line of direction. It may be placed *at* the center of gravity, or at some

point *above* it, or at some point *below* it. Fig. 5 shows
a disk of metal supported in these three ways.

Fig. 5.

Describe three kinds of equilibrium.—When all
parts of a body are balanced it is said to be in equilibrium.
Now when the support is at the center of gravity, as
shown in the middle disk of the figure, the body is said
to be in *indifferent equilibrium*, because it will rest as
well in one position as another.

When the support is placed above the center of gravity,
as in the disk at the right hand, the body is said to be in
stable equilibrium, because it will not rest as well in any
other position.

When the support is placed exactly below the center of
gravity, as in the disk at the left hand, the body is said to
be in *unstable equilibrium*, because the slightest force will
push it over.

**That a body may stand, where must the line of
direction pass ?**—If the line of direction passes through
any point in the base on which the body is placed, the
body will stand, but if this line passes outside of the base,

the body must fall. The leaning cylinder in Fig. 4 does not fall, because the line of direction passes through the base, and hence the center of gravity is supported; but if it should lean a little more this line would pass outside the base, and the cylinder would tip over. A table stands very firm because it is not easy to tip it so far that the line of direction would pass outside the base.

Carriages may lean considerably to one side without overturning (Fig. 6), but an accident is sure to happen if

Fig. 6.

they lean so far as to throw the line of direction beyond the lower side of the wheel.

Upon what does the stability of a body depend?—Now some bodies stand more firmly than others, and in looking for the reason we find that the stability of a body depends upon two things. The first of these is, the height of the center of gravity above the base.

A wagon loaded with hay overturns easily, while if loaded with stone it would pass the same spot in the road with perfect safety. The center of gravity of the load of hay is so much higher, that to lean a little throws the line

of direction beyond the wheel.   The higher the center of
gravity of any body is, the more unstable will it be.

What else influences the stability of a body ?—
The size of the base is the second thing that influences
the stability of a body.   It will of course be more difficult
to tip the line of direction beyond a large base than beyond a small one.   A narrow boat overturns more easily
than a wide one, or, to mention an example which you
may see at any time, a thick book will stand upon its end
more firmly than a thin one of the same height.

We see, then, that the lower the center of gravity and
the broader the base, the firmer will the body stand.

Mention illustrations of these principles.—Illustrations of these principles of center of gravity are among
the most common affairs of life.   Indeed, we unconsciously
apply them in almost every motion and position of our
own bodies.

When standing, the *base* upon which the body rests is
the space between the feet; the center of gravity must be

Fig. 7.

kept over this base or the person will fall.   In carrying a
pail of water we unconsciously lean to the other side, and

if the load is very heavy we at the same time stretch out the opposite arm (Fig. 7). The pack-peddler leans forward, for if he did not the heavy load would throw the center of gravity behind his feet and he would tumble backward.

What illustration does the showman furnish?—The showman offers a gold coin to the boy who will stand with his heels pressed against the wall of a room and then. pick it from the floor in front of him without falling. He is perfectly safe in making the offer. For no one can stoop without falling, unless when he throws his head forward he can, at the same time, throw some other part of his body backward far enough to keep his center of gravity over his feet. He can not do this with his heels pressed against a wall.

Why is a child so long learning to walk?—When we think how narrow the base is on which a child must stand, being just the space on the floor between its little feet, and then how high is the center of gravity of his . body, we need not wonder that he is so long a time in learning to walk. The many falls and bruises which the little one gets mark his failures in the art of supporting the center of gravity always over the base.

How may we try the experiment?—Let one who has forgotten how hard it was for him to learn to walk refresh his memory by trying to walk on stilts. Skill in this, like that of the child in walking, needs only the power to keep the center of gravity of the body, every moment, over some point in the base.

LIQUIDS.

How do liquids differ from solids?—The molecules of every solid substance are held together so that the body will keep whatever form you may choose to give it; but in water the molecules are held together with such feeble force that they can move among themselves with the greatest ease, and you can not give it any shape but that of the vessel which holds it.

Water and other substances, in which cohesion is so slight that the molecules move freely among themselves, are called liquids.

Is there any cohesion in liquids?—Still the cohesion in a liquid is strong enough to be detected. Look again at Fig. 2, and notice that the water would not be lifted under the disk, as it is there shown to be, unless the particles of water cling to each other. This shows cohesion among them. The drop of dew collected upon a leaf (Fig. 8) shows cohesion in water, for what else could hold the parts of the drop together?

Fig. 8.

How can we judge of its strength?—To get a bet-

ter idea of the force of cohesion in water, we may watch
it dripping from some support. A drop grows larger
while clinging to its support, until at last it breaks away.
The *weight of the drop* just at the moment when it breaks
away is just enough to pull the molecules of water apart,
and *measures the cohesion* in the liquid. The liquid in
which there is the greatest cohesion will give the largest
drops.

Is water compressible ?—A famous experiment was
made at Florence about a hundred years ago to find out
whether water could be compressed. A hollow globe of
gold was filled with water, and then the opening sealed so
very tight that no water could pass it. An enormous
pressure was then put upon the globe, when, to the surprise of all, the water oozed through the pores of the
metal. This experiment seemed to prove that water was
not compressible. But more careful experiments have
since shown that water is compressible. It is in so
slight a degree that the Fiorentine experiment was too
rude to show it at all. It needs a pressure of 15 lbs.
upon every square inch of the surface of the vessel in
which the water is held to compress the fluid .0000503 of
its bulk.

Is water elastic ?—The instant that the pressure is
removed from the compressed water it springs back to its
former bulk, and this proves it to be elastic.

What is more remarkable, it springs back with exactly
as much force as was exerted to compress it. When compressed only .0000503 of its bulk it will spring back with
a force of 15 lbs. to a square inc. Now when a body
springing back restores all the force that compressed it,

it is said to be perfectly elastic. Water and other liquids are perfectly elastic.

What shows the downward pressure of water? —The downward pressure of water is shown by its weight. To lift a pailful of water you must overcome its downward pressure. This may tax your strength severely, because, if the pail holds one cubic foot of the liquid, you must lift a weight of $62\frac{1}{2}$ lbs.; a cubic foot of water weighs $62\frac{1}{2}$ lbs.

Does water exert pressure upward?—To learn whether water presses upward as well as downward the following experiment (Fig. 9) may be tried. A plate of

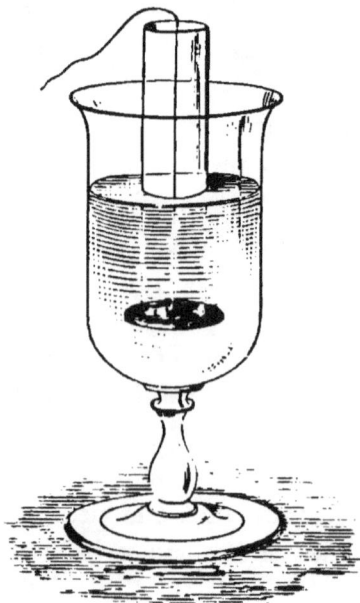

Fig. 9.

metal is hung from the end of a string, which is passed through a glass tube open at both ends. By means of this string the plate of metal may be held tightly against the lower end of the tube. Now if this end of the tube is pushed down into a vessel of water, the string may be dropped and the plate of metal will still stay up against the glass. By a moment's thought you see that it must be the water that holds the heavy metal up, and that to do this it must exert an upward pressure.

Does water exert pressure sidewise?—The same

experiment shows that water exerts a pressure sidewise, for you may find that the water is gradually pushed side-wise between the plate and the end of the tube, slowly filling the tube with water.

In what direction does water exert pressure?— In fact, water and other liquids, when at rest, exert press-ure in all directions. And another fact should be remem-bered; it is, that the pressure at any point is *equal* in all directions. If, for example, there is at any point a down-ward pressure of 10 lbs. there will be, at the same time, a pressure of 10 lbs. upward and sidewise, and indeed in every possible direction.

The pressure of water in several directions at once is very well shown in Fig. 10.

Fig. 10.

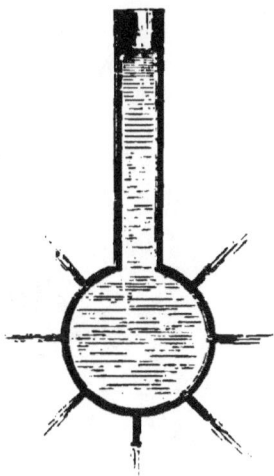

Why is the surface of wa-ter at rest always level?—It is because water presses equally in all directions that a body of water can not be quiet unless its upper surface is level.

· Let us explain this more fully. The molecules of water move so easily that if the pressure in one direction is never so little more than in another, the liquid will move. Now if the downward pressures at all points are equal, all the other pressures must be equal too, and the water will not move, but the downward pressures will not be equal at all points unless the surface of the water is level, and for this reason the water can not rest unless its surface is level.

The wind may cover the surface of the sea with ripples

or lash it into billows; but let the wind be hushed, and the ripples or billows will gradually' sink into a surface smoother than that of the most polished mirror, just because the pressure in all directions can not be made equal without.

Will the shape of the vessel make any difference?—No matter how irregular the form of a vessel may be, all parts of the surface of the water in it must be at the same height, or in other words level. The vessel shown in Fig. 11 has a very irregular shape. There is

Fig. 11.

first the large vase at the left hand, then the horizontal tube, and finally the tubes reaching upward from the last; yet it is all one vessel, because the water can pass freely from one part to another.

If water is poured into the vase it will rise just as fast in the tubes, and will at last stand at the same height in all parts, as the picture shows.

How are cities supplied with water?—It is on

this principle that many cities are supplied with water. Water from the streams of the country around is led into a reservoir where its surface will be higher than the city. A large pipe is then laid under-ground, reaching from the reservoir down to the city, and branches from it are laid under the streets. From these main pipes·a branch goes into each house which is to receive the water, and reaches up to the room where the water is to be drawn. Now the water will rise in these pipes as high as the surface of that in the reservoir, if they will allow it to do so, and, of course, if one be opened anywhere below that level the water will flow from it.

How are fountains produced?—If the pipe which is bringing water from a reservoir does not rise as high as the reservoir, the water will spout upward in the form of a fountain. In Fig. 11 one of the tubes is shorter than the others, but the water rises almost as high as it does in them : being thrown into the air instead of rising in a pipe, we call it a fountain.

Upon what does the pressure of water on the bottom of the vessel which holds it depend?— Suppose the bottoms of two vessels are the same in size, but that one vessel is twice as high as the other. When both are filled with water it is found that there will be just twice as much pressure on the bottom of the highest. If one is three times as high as the other, the pressure on its bottom will be three times as great.

The pressure upon the bottom of a vessel·of water is always just in proportion to the height of·the water.

Does not the shape of the vessel make a difference?—We may take vessels of very different shapes, but if they are filled with water to the same height, and if their bottoms are of the same size, the pressure on the bottom will be the same in all. Suppose, for example, that each vessel has a bottom whose surface is ten square inches: one of them may be just as large at the top as at the bottom, another may be larger at the top, and another smaller; but when they are filled to the same height with water the pressure upon the bottoms will be alike in all.

The pressure upon a bottom of given size depends *entirely* upon the height of the water above it.

How may a little water exert very great pressure ?—We may now notice a curious fact, which seems at first to be impossible. *A very small quantity of water may exert an enormous pressure.*

Fig. 12 shows how this may be proved. In the first place, a very tight cask is filled with water and a tall tube is afterward screwed into the top. By filling this tube with water the cask, unless uncommonly strong, will be broken asunder. The very small quantity of water in the tube, no more than a child could lift, exerts a pressure strong enough to break the staves of the cask.

How can this be explained?—Suppose the end of the tube is $\frac{1}{50}$ of a square inch, and that the tube is high enough to hold a pound of water. The pressure on $\frac{1}{50}$ of an inch would be one pound, and on a whole inch it would be 50 lbs. And since water presses equally in all directions there would be 50 lbs. pressure on *every* square inch of the inside surface of the cask. Such a pressure is more than the cask can bear.

Would any other equal pressure have the same effect?—Any other pressure equal to the weight of the column of water in the tube would have the same effect. The pressure of your hand, or of a pound-weight of metal, might take the place of the pound of water in the tube:

Fig. 12.

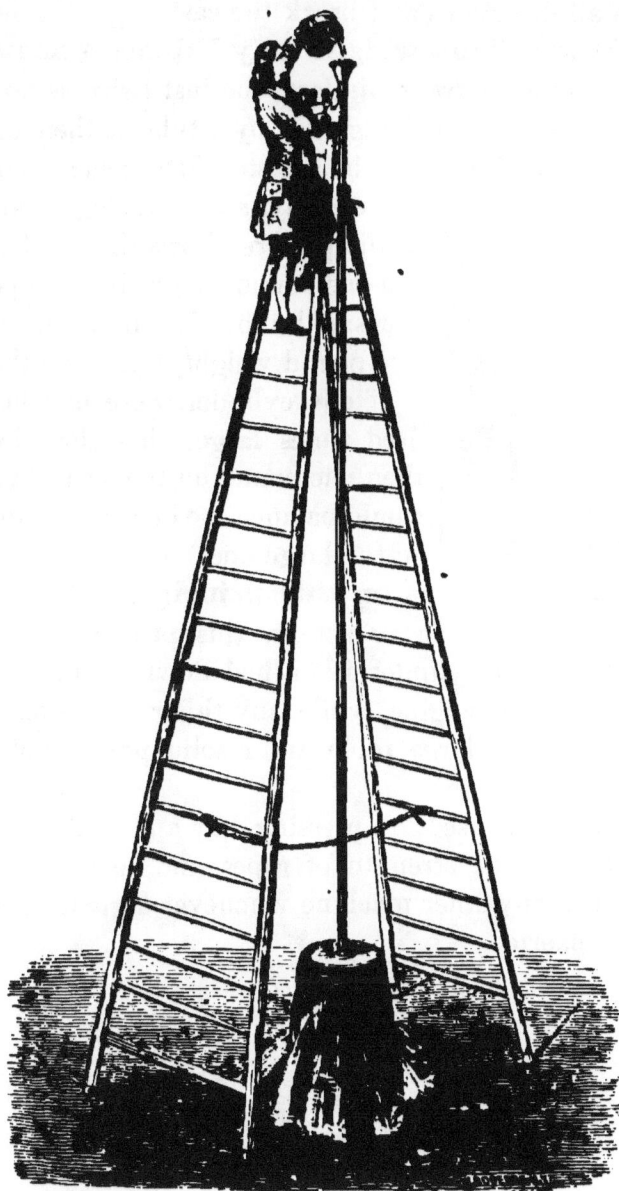

the pressure, exerted in any way, would be transmitted equally in all directions and break the cask.

Show how a light weight may balance a heavy one.—Now suppose two cylinders, one just twice as large as the other, to be joined together by a tube at their bottoms (Fig. 13), and let there be a piston fitting each cylin-

Fig. 13.

der exactly, and carrying a table as the picture shows them. Now if a one-pound weight be put upon the small table it will balance a two-pound weight upon the other.

If one cylinder were one hundred times larger than the other, then one pound on the small table would balance one hundred pounds on the large one.

What machine acts on this principle?—The hydrostatic press is made to act on this principle. The piston in the small cylinder is pushed down by hand, or perhaps by a steam-engine, while any thing to be pressed is put between the large table and a solid pressure-plate built above it.

This machine is used for pressing hay and cotton into bales, for testing the strength of ropes, and, in a word, it is preferred to any other machine whenever a great pressure is to be exerted.

GASES.

How do gases differ from liquids?—In water and in other liquids there is a slight degree of cohesion, but in air and other gases there is no cohesion at all. The molecules of air are trying to get just as far away from each other as possible at all times; and this is true also of all bodies in the form of air, or, as they are called, gases.

Air is the most common of all gases, and on this account it is used to illustrate the properties of this class of bodies.

Is the air expansible?—An easy and pretty experiment will teach us whether air can be expanded. Take a small vial having in it a little colored water, and fasten into its neck an air-tight cork, through which a small tube just reaches into the bottle. This tube should be several inches long. If the vial be held bottom upward the colored water will not run into the tube, but if the lips be applied to the lower end of the tube, and the air be drawn out, the colored water will quickly run down. This shows that the air above the water in the vial expands to push the water out.

In what other way is the air of the vial expanded?—If, instead of taking the air out of the tube, you gently warm the vial, you will see the colored liquid move out of the vial and down the tube. In this experiment the air is expanded by heat.

Boys sometimes amuse themselves by bursting balloons or bladders filled with air by warming them. They thus illustrate the expansibility of air, for the air when heated tries to fill more room than it did when cold, and in trying to get larger bursts the balloon with a loud report like a gun.

Fig. 14.

Is air compressible ?—If we take a cylinder with a piston fitting it air-tight (Fig. 14), we may easily push the piston down some distance into the cylinder. No air gets out, but the piston, while going down, crowds the air along before it until the cylinder may be less than half full. By greater force than can be given by the hand alone the piston may be crowded down until the cylinder may be less than a hundredth or a thousandth part full.

Is air elastic ?—Compressed air will spring back to its original bulk when the pressure is taken away, and this shows that it is *elastic.*

It is also found that air after being compressed will spring back with just as much force as was put upon it; this shows it to be *perfectly* elastic.

Does air have weight ?—A thin globe made of glass or metal is weighed when full of air (Fig. 15). The air is then taken out of it by means of an air-pump, soon to be described, and the empty globe is weighed. The globe weighs more when full of air than when empty, and this proves that air has weight.

If the globe will hold 100 cubic inches of air, it will

weigh about 31 grains less when empty, and this shows that 100 cubic inches weigh about 31 grains.

Does gravitation act upon air?—The weight of air, like the weight of wood or iron, is caused by the attraction of gravitation. Gravitation acts upon the invisible air in just the same way that it does upon water or upon oil, only its action is not so strong.

Fig. 15.

Try this experiment: into a tall glass jar (Fig. 16) or even a goblet put first some water, and then pour in some oil; the oil will lie on top of the water. Afterward, if you can have some mercury you will be able to pour it

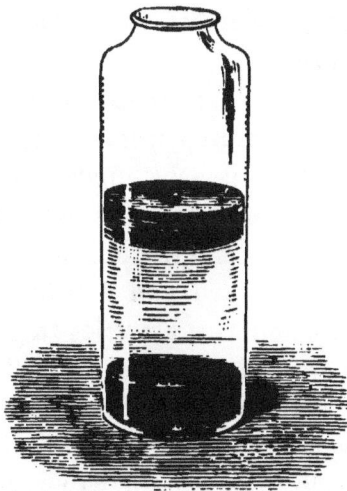

Fig. 16.

into the jar carefully without disturbing the other liquids. The mercury will go to the bottom and form a layer under the others.

Now there are *four* substances in the jar, arranged in layers. There is first mercury, then water, then oil, and then *air*. And they are in this order because gravitation is strongest on mercury, weaker on water, weaker yet on oil, and weakest on air.

For a similar reason the water of the sea is above the rocks and then the atmosphere above the water; but if gravitation did not act upon air at all, the atmosphere would leave the earth entirely and fly off into space beyond.

In what directions does air exert pressure ?—The pressure of the air may be shown in a very simple way. Cork one end of a lamp-chimney, and stretch a piece of caoutchouc over the other. Put a piece of pipe-stem tightly through the cork, and the apparatus is finished. Now with the lips at the pipe-stem, take the air out of the chimney and you will see the caoutchouc pushed into it. There is nothing outside to push it into the tube but the air, and so the experiment shows the pressure of the air.

Now hold the tube upward or downward, or in any direction whatever, and the caoutchouc will be pressed in as before; and hence we see that the air presses in *all directions.*

It is also found by experiment that the pressure of air in all directions is equal. In this respect air and water are alike.

The finest illustrations of the pressure of the air may be given by means of the air-pump.

Describe the air-pump.—In this instrument there is a cylinder (C, Fig. 17), with a tube leading from the bottom of it. The other end of this tube is bent upward so as to pass through a horizontal plate of metal, P. At the end of this tube, in the cylinder, there is a little door or valve, as it is called, which opens upward, and will open for air to go up, but will shut when the air tries to go down again. In the cylinder there is a piston, and in this there is another valve which opens upward. The plate, P, is so smooth that a glass vessel, R, open at the bottom, will stand upon it and fit so closely that no air can pass between them. This vessel, or any other from which air is to be taken, is called a *receiver.*

Explain the action of the pump.—When the piston is lifted the air in the receiver, R, will expand, and a part

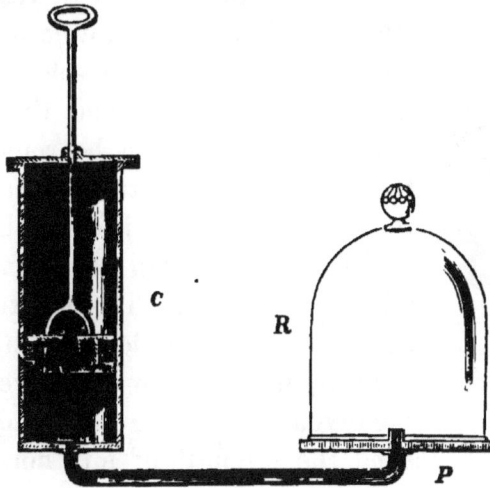

Fig. 17.

of it will go through the valve at the bottom of the cylinder. When the piston is pushed down again, the air in the cylinder will push its way through the valve in the piston. When the piston is lifted again, the air above it is lifted out of the instrument entirely, while another part of the air in the receiver comes through the valve into the cylinder. And in this way every upward motion of the piston pumps a part of the air out from the receiver.

The air can be so nearly pumped out, or *exhausted*, as it is usually called, that there will not be enough left to lift the very delicate valves of the instrument.

How will the receiver show the pressure of the air?—After the air has been pumped out of the receiver, it will be found impossible to lift it away from the pump-plate. The outside air presses so heavily upon it that if the receiver is lifted the pump will rise with it.

How may the pressure be shown by the Magde-burg cups?—Fig. 18 shows the Magdeburg cups. These cups are made of metal, and their edges are so smooth that they will fit each other air-tight. The lower one may be screwed upon the pump-plate, the other then placed upon it and the air taken out. They may then be removed from the pump without letting the air get into them, and when this is done, the pressure of the outside air will hold them together with great force. The illustrious Otto de Guericke of Magdeburg, who invented the air-pump, and to whom we also owe the invention of these cups, made a pair so large that it needed the strength of four horses to pull them apart.

Fig. 18.

How may the pressure be shown by the fountain in vacuo?—The pressure of air is shown by a still more beautiful experiment, represented in Fig. 19. A tall glass receiver, R, made air-tight, has a tube passing through the bottom. The lower end of this tube may be screwed upon the plate of the air-pump: the other end reaches some distance into the vessel. After the air is exhausted from the receivers, if the lower end of the tube is placed in water and the valve opened, an elegant fountain will be thrown up inside by the pressure of the air upon the water outside.

How may the upward pressure of air be shown? —We do not need an air-pump to show the upward pressure of air. Just take a common bottle and fill it to the brim with water; then place a piece of paper over its mouth, and while you hold the paper with one hand, turn the bottle bottom upward with the other. You may now let go of the paper and the water will not run out of the

Fig. 19.

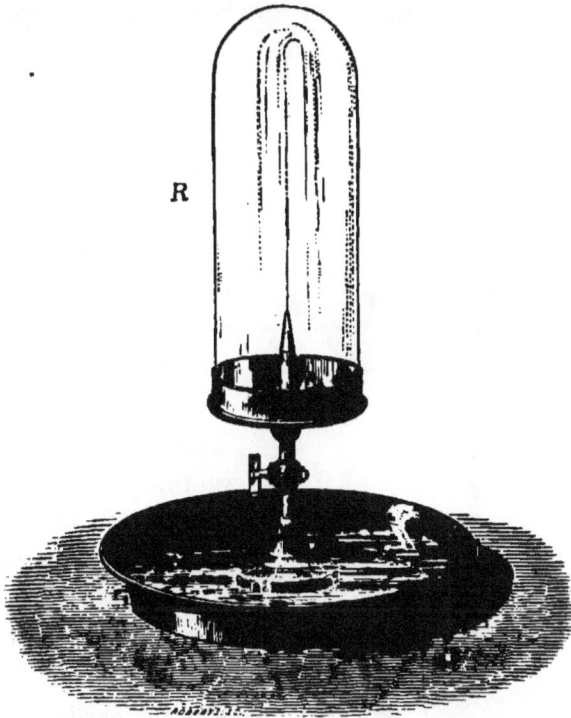

bottle. The water and the paper are both held up by the upward pressure of the air. If the neck of the bottle is very small, the paper need not be used.

How may the downward pressure be easily shown?—Take a tall bottle with a wide mouth, and sink it in a vessel of water, and when full of the liquid lift it gradually with its bottom upward until its neck only is covered. The bottle will still be full of water. The pressure of the air on the water in the vessel pushes the liquid up into the bottle and holds it there.

It is the pressure of air which also drives water through

a glass tube or a straw when, one end being in the liquid, the lips are applied to the other end. All that the lips do is to take the air out of the tube above the water.

How high a column of water will the pressure of the air sustain?—The water will be sustained to a height of about 34 feet by this pressure of the air.

Fig. 20.

How high a column of mercury?—A column of mercury about 30 inches high will weigh as much as a column of water 34 feet high if they are of the same size. Therefore, a column of mercury only 30 inches high will be supported by the pressure of the air

Can we prove this by experiment?—The pictures show how this can be easily proved by experiment. A glass tube more than 30 inches long is taken. One end of it is closed, the other open. It is first filled with mercury, and then the open end is shut with the finger, while the tube is turned, closed end upward, as shown in Fig. 20. The open end is then put into a dish of mercury and the finger taken away. The mercury will no longer quite fill the tube, but will sink so as to leave the upper part empty, as shown in Fig. 21. The air-pressure supports this column of mercury, and the height measures about 30 inches.

How much pressure does the atmosphere exert upon a square inch?—A column of mercury one inch square and thirty inches high will weigh 15 lbs. To balance 15 lbs. of mercury in the tube, or to keep it from falling out, would need another pressure of 15 lbs., and since the air does this we know that it must be exerting a pressure of 15 *pounds to the square inch.*

Fig. 21.

Air is lighter than the lightest down, but reaching above us to a height of many miles, the quantity in all must be immense. It covers every thing upon the earth, and presses upon each square inch of the surface of every thing with a force of 15 lbs. The total pressure upon each one of our bodies is said to be about 20,000 lbs. We are able to bear this great pressure without feeling it, because it is so exactly equal in all directions, and because every point on the body, bearing its own share, divides the labor so justly that no point is burdened.

Is the pressure of the atmosphere always alike?
—By watching the column of mercury in the tube, Fig.
21, it will be found to be higher at some times than at
others. This must be because the pressure of the atmosphere is not always the same. It is sometimes a little
more than 15 lbs. to the inch and sometimes a little
less.

How does the pressure vary with the weather?
—In bright, clear weather the atmosphere is heavier than
when storms or clouds prevail. Hence the column of
mercury will be higher in fair weather than in foul
weather; and by watching the changes in the height of
the mercury column we may judge something of what the
character of the weather is to be.

How does the pressure vary with the height?—
At the level of the sea the column of mercury stands 30
inches high. A gentleman by the name of Pascal, in
France, with a tube and cistern of mercury, traveled up a
mountain-side to find what effect, if any, would be produced
upon the column. As he climbed the mountain higher
and higher, he found that the mercury sank lower and
lower in the tube. We learn from his experiment that the
pressure of the atmosphere is less as the height is greater.

May we not know this without experiment?—
Indeed, no experiment is needed to prove this, for it is
very clear that when going up we leave a part of the
atmosphere below us, and there being then less above us,
the pressure exerted must be less.

What is the Barometer?—Now the barometer is an
instrument which shows the changes in the pressure of
the atmosphere. It consists of a tube with a cistern of
mercury, like that shown in Fig. 21, placed in a framework of wood or metal which protects it from injury. A

scale placed behind the tube shows the height of the mercury column.

How does this instrument toretell changes in the weather?—By the *motion* of the mercury up or down we may judge something of the future character of the weather. If we see the mercury rising, we may expect fair weather: if the mercury falls, we may expect foul weather.

How is it used to find the height of mountains?—From the sea-level to the top of Mont Blanc is a height of about 15,000 feet. In going to the summit, the mercury column falls about 15 inches. From this, and other observations like this, it appears that the mercury sinks about one inch for every thousand feet the barometer is taken upward. To get the height of a mountain, then, we may count 1,000 feet for every inch through which the mercury falls in being carried to the summit.

This rule will not give the exact height, owing to things which we will not now try to explain, but when all things are taken into account in making the calculations, the height of a mountain may be calculated by the barometer perhaps more easily and exactly than by any other method.

Describe the lifting-pump.—In this very common and useful instrument the pressure of the atmosphere is

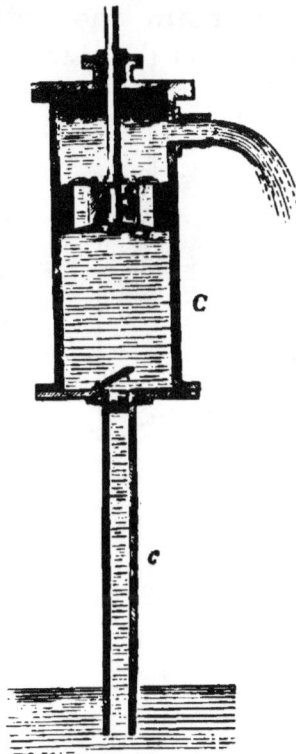

Fig. 22.

made to lift water from a well or cistern. Its parts and their action are very well shown in Fig. 22. It consists of two cylinders, one above the other, the upper one, C, being often much larger than the other, c, which reaches down into the well. Where these cylinders join each other there is a little door, or valve, which opens upward, and will allow water to go up, but will not let it go down again. In the upper cylinder there is a piston which may be lifted or pushed down by the handle of the pump. In this piston there is a valve, or, it may be, more than one, which opens upward.

Explain the action of the pump.—By the first strokes of the piston the air is taken out of the cylinders,

Fig 23.

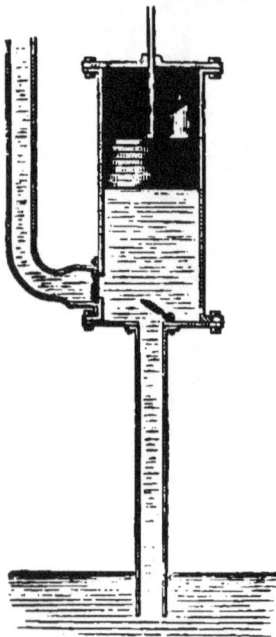

and then the pressure of the atmosphere upon the water in the well pushes the water up into the pump just as it will push water up into a straw or other tube when the air is drawn out at the top by applying the lips. After the air has been all taken out, the water will fill the pump full to the spout, and then every time the piston is raised it will lift a portion of water out at the spout, while more is pushed in at the bottom by the air to take its place.

Describe the force-pump.—Fig. 23 shows a kind of pump which is used for throwing water to greater heights. It is called the *force-pump*. The spout is at the bottom of the upper cylinder instead of near the top of it, as in the lifting-pump, and instead of having any valve in the piston there is one opening into the spout. In other respects it is like the lifting-pump.

Explain its action.—When the piston is lifted the atmosphere pushes water up into the upper cylinder. When the piston is pushed down the water is pushed through the valve into the spout. This spout may reach even to the top of a house, and the water will go higher by each stroke of the piston until it reaches the top and runs over. A *jet* of water would be thrown out by each downward stroke of the piston, but if a *steady stream* is wanted, the spout leads into an air-chamber where the water condenses the air. This condensed air exerts a steady pressure on the water in the chamber and throws it out in a steady stream.

The fire-engine is a form of force-pump. In the steam fire-engine the piston is moved by the power of steam.

What is the siphon?—In Fig. 24, the tube from which the water appears to be running is a siphon. The instrument is used to pass a liquid from one vessel to another. The siphon is never any thing more than a bent tube, one arm being longer than the other.

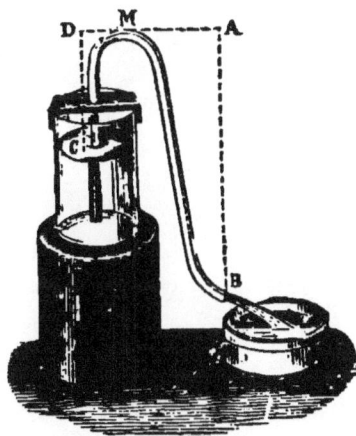
Fig. 24.

How is it used?—When the siphon is to be used, it must first be filled with water, and then the end of the long arm is closed with the finger, while the short arm is put into the liquid in the vessel. The moment the finger is removed, the liquid will begin to flow up the short arm, over the bend and out at the end of the long arm; nor will it stop running until the end of the short arm is uncovered, or until the liquid is as high in the second vessel as in the one from which it runs.

Explain its action.—It often at first seems a mystery why the liquid should run upward through the short arm and out from the other; but we shall see that the forces that push it in that direction are stronger than those that push the other way.

To push it out through the long arm there is, *first*, the weight of the liquid in that arm, and, *second*, the pressure of the air on the water in the vessel.

To keep it in, there is, *first*, the weight of the water in the short arm, and, *second*, the pressure of the air upward against the water at the end of the long arm.

Now the first two forces are stronger than the last two, because the weight of the water in the long arm is greater than of that in the short arm; and the water runs in the direction of the greater force.

MOTION.

Can bodies move themselves ? — Animals can move from place to place, because they have the power of will, and their bodies must obey it ; but that a book or a block of stone should of its own accord move out of its place, we pronounce to be impossible. Such bodies of matter can move only as they are either *pushed* or *pulled.* The ship, for example, is pushed along by wind : a train of cars is pulled along by a steam-engine. A stone falls to the ground because it is pulled down by the attraction of the earth, and the smoke rises because it is pushed upward by the heavier air.

A body at rest would rest forever if it were neither pushed nor pulled by some force outside of itself.

Can bodies stop themselves ? — A moving ship will not stop suddenly when the sails are taken down. The water finally stops it ; no one ever thinks of saying that the ship stops itself. A train of cars moves along some distance after the steam has been cut off : it is finally stopped by the friction of the wheels as they rub upon their axles and upon the track, together with other obstacles which it meets ; it does not stop itself. A horse and his rider are moving along together ; let the horse suddenly stop, and his rider is plunged over his head ; the man can not stop himself.

We learn from these observations that a body in motion

3*

would move forever if it were not stopped by some force outside of itself.

Can a body change the direction of its motion?—When a ball is struck with a bat, it flies in the direction of the blow, and in no other, unless turned aside by some other force.

The same thing appears to be true of all other motions, for who ever saw a moving body suddenly of its own accord start off in another direction! A body in motion would move forever in a straight line unless turned aside by some force outside itself.

What is the first law of motion?—We may now state, in very few words, what we have thus far learned about motion, as follows:

A body at rest would rest forever, or if in motion would move forever in a straight line, unless kept from doing so by some force outside of itself.

This principle is called the first law of motion.

Why then does not a stone move in a straight line when thrown from the hand?—When a stone is thrown in a horizontal direction, we find that instead of going along in that direction, it very soon flies lower and lower, until at length it strikes the ground. It would move in a straight line if the attraction of the earth did not pull it to the ground.

Are other motions caused by more than one force?—If the wind blows while the rain falls we see the drops coming obliquely down to the ground. Gravitation alone would bring them vertically through the air, but the wind at the same time pushes them sidewise; their motion is due to these two forces.

Now, the more examples of motion we examine, the more certain we become that the motions of bodies are generally caused by two or more forces acting upon them at the same time.

Does each force prcduce as much effect as if it acted alone ?—Here is an experiment that any one can try for himself while studying this subject. Put a ball at one corner of a table. You may snap it with the fingers of one hand and make it roll along the side of the table, and if you afterward snap it with the fingers of the other hand you may make it roll across the end; but if you skillfully snap it with the fingers of both hands at once, it will follow neither the side nor the end, but you will see it dart obliquely across to the opposite corner.

If one hand would roll the ball the whole *length of the table* in *one second*, and if the other would roll it *across the end* in *one second*, then, when both hands were used at once, the ball will roll to the *opposite* corner in *exactly one second*. But to get to this opposite corner, the ball must go the whole length and the whole width of the table both at once; so that each force causes just as much motion in the second of time as if it were acting alone.

Give another example.—The swift motion of a cannon-ball is caused by the explosion of gunpowder, but gravitation is at the same time pulling the ball down toward the ground. If the ball is shot in a horizontal direction it will strike the ground at the same time it would if dropped from the mouth of the gun. The force of gravitation pulls the ball downward through the same distance while it is moving horizontally as it would in the same time if falling vertically.

Suppose the ball shot directly upward.—A ball will fall about 16 feet in the first second after it starts. Now suppose a ball shot directly upward, and that the force of the powder would be strong enough to send it up

100 feet in the first second: the ball will only rise 84 feet. The attraction of gravitation which would make it fall 16 feet if it were not for the powder, will cut off just 16 feet from its ascent.

What is the second law of motion?—From such facts as these we infer that:

A force will cause the same amount of motion, and in the same direction, whether the body it acts upon be at rest or already in motion.

This principle is called the second law of motion.

What is meant by action and reaction?—He who strikes the table with his hand gets a blow from the table in return, as he very well knows by the pain it occasions when the blow is heavy. The hand *acts* upon the table and the table *reacts* upon the hand. Whenever two bodies act upon each other, the effect of one of them is called *action*, that of the other is called *reaction*.

A bullet may perhaps fracture a stone against which it is fired, but the bullet will be flattened, showing that the stone has returned the blow. The bullet acts upon the stone and the stone reacts upon the bullet.

Are action and reaction in the same direction?—When a book lies upon the table it presses *downward*, but the table is at the same time pressing *upward* to keep the book from going to the floor. Action and reaction must always be in opposite directions.

Which is the stronger?—Take the case of the book on the table: the action of the book downward, or its pressure, is just equal to its weight. If the table should react with a force *greater* than the weight of the book, it would throw the book upward; if with *less* force, the book would be able to break through it: it can be neither greater nor less, because the book is at rest. In every other case as well as this, action and reaction are equal.

What is the third law of motion?—From what has just now been said we may gather this general statement:

Every action must be followed by an opposite and equal reaction.

This principle is called the third law of motion.

What is an impulsive force?—When a bullet is shot from a gun, the force of the gunpowder acts upon it only for a single moment when it starts. A force which acts for a moment only is called an *impulsive force.*

Other examples are common enough. When a ball is hit with a bat, the force of the blow is spent upon the ball in an instant. And at the moment when a stone leaves the hand that throws it, the force of the hand is spent. Both of these are impulsive forces.

What do we notice about the motion caused by impulsive forces?—We notice that the motions produced by these impulsive forces are all alike in one thing at least: the velocity is greatest at the beginning. The speed of the bullet is greatest at the moment when it leaves the gun, and grows less and less until it is stopped entirely. And in the case of the ball struck with a bat, and of the stone thrown from the hand, motion is swiftest at the beginning and gradually grows slower.

Why do these motions grow slower?—It would not be so if it were not for the resistance of the air. The resistance of the air which hinders the snow-flakes so that they can not fall like rain-drops or hail-stones, also hinders the motion of every thing else.

Cut a leaf of paper into pieces an inch in length and half as wide; toss them upward into the quiet air of the room and watch their slow and curious motions to the floor : if it were not for the air which hinders them they would fall like bullets.

The air hinders the motion of heavy bodies, and the faster they move the more it will affect it. Even the motion of cannon-balls is rapidly lessened by the resistance of the air.

Now if there were no air nor other resistances the motion caused by an impulsive force would not grow less. The moving body would pass over equal distances in equal times, or in other words, its motion would be uniform.

What is a constant force?—The force of the hand which tosses a stone upward into the air is an impulsive force, but gravitation which brings it down again is not. Never for a single instant does gravitation cease to act upon the falling stone. and on this account it is called a *constant force*. A constant force is one whose action is all the time alike.

What do we notice about the motion it produces?—The motion of a falling body is swifter and swifter the farther it falls. This is true not only of motion caused by gravitation, but of motion caused by any constant force whatever ; the velocity increases while the force is acting.

How do the air and other resistances affect this motion?—In this case also the resistance of the air hinders the motion, and it hinders it more and more as the velocity is greater. In fact, the motion of a body falling from a great height may become so swift that the resistance of the air will be as strong as the force of gravitation itself, and after that moment the motion will be uniform.

It is just so with a train of cars. The power of the steam starts it and for a little time makes it go faster and faster, but the motion soon becomes uniform because the many resistances which the train meets soon equals the power of the steam.

The motion of a sail-boat increases at first, but very soon the resistance of the water becomes so strong that it needs the whole force of the wind to overcome it, and after that the boat sails on at a uniform rate.

In what kind of a path will an arrow go?—If an arrow is shot from the bow directly upward, it will go up in a straight line and its motion back again will also be in a straight line. If, however, the arrow be fired in any other direction its path will be a curve instead of being straight.

Why will the path of the arrow be curved?—It is easy to see that there are two forces acting on the arrow. There is, first, the force of the bow which sends it forward, and then, second, the force of gravitation which pulls it toward the ground. The bow would send it in a straight line, but gravitation is all the time pulling it down out of that line. The arrow obeys both of these forces at once, going forward and downward at the same time, its direction changing a little all the time. For this reason the path of the arrow is curved.

In any case, if a body moves in a curved path it is being acted on by two forces, and one of these, at least, must constantly act.

Give another example.—We may make an easy experiment to illustrate this statement more fully. Tie a string to the stem of an apple and make the apple swing around the hand in a circle. You can feel the apple pulling as if struggling to get away from the hand, and should you let go your hold of the string the apple would dart off in a straight line in just whatever direction it happened at the moment to be going.

What two forces make the apple move in the

circle ?—There is one force, we notice, which is trying to move the apple in a straight line, and the string is another force which is pulling it out of that line every moment.

By these two forces acting together the apple is moved in a circle.

What are the centrifugal and centripetal forces? —Now one of the two forces by which curved motion is produced has been called the *centrifugal* force, and the other the *centripetal* force. The one which would send the body away in a straight line is the centrifugal force; that which pulls it out of the straight line is the centripetal force.

What familiar examples of the action of these forces?—The stone in a sling, at the moment when it is set at liberty, darts off in a line as straight as the path of an arrow or a bullet: but before it is set at liberty, the sling-cord pulls it out of that line and keeps it moving in a circle.

A wet mop, made to turn swiftly on its handle as an axis, throws the water in all directions and soon dries itself. It is the centrifugal force which sends the water away. And this illustrates what we sometimes see among animals. Sheep, for example, in wet weather throw the water off themselves by shaking their fleeces in a kind of half rotary motion. Water-dogs on coming to land dry themselves in the same way.

"A loaded stage-coach running south and turning suddenly to the east or west, strews its passengers on the south side of the road. A man on horseback when turning a corner leans much toward the corner in order to overcome the centrifugal force which would throw him away from it."

A carriage-wheel turning swiftly often throws the dirt in straight lines from its circumference. In the same way, were it not for the attraction of gravitation, all bodies on the face of the earth would be thrown out into the heavens by the centrifugal force due to the rotation of the earth upon its axis.

The earth is moving in an orbit which is almost a circle, the diameter of which is about 190,000,000 miles, and it is going at the rate of about 68,000 miles an hour. At every moment during this wonderful journey the earth is struggling to fly away in a straight line, but the powerful attraction of the sun is the strong arm which constantly pulls it out of this line into the graceful curve through which it flies.

Describe the pendulum.—In Fig. 25 we notice a ball B hung from a fixed point A by means of a cord.

Fig. 25.

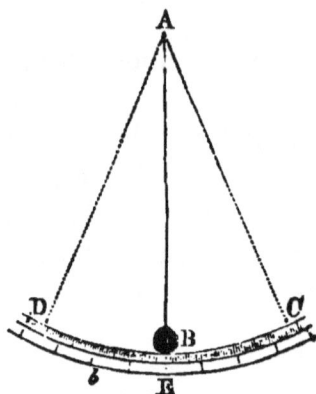

This ball represents a pendulum: any body hung from a fixed point, under which it may swing from side to side, backward and forward, is a pendulum.

If such a ball were pulled aside and then dropped it would swing for a long time. You can easily try the experiment by hanging an apple in the same way and making it swing.

What is meant by vibration and amplitude ?—If the pendulum (Fig. 25) is lifted to C it will swing to D, a point almost as far on the other side, and then return. It will keep on moving back and forth in this arc until the resistance of the air finally stops it at B, the place from which it first started. Its *motion* from one end of its arc to the other is called a *vibration*, and the *distance* from one end of its arc to the other is called its *amplitude*.

Does the time of one vibration depend upon amplitude ?—The distance through which the pendulum swings makes very little difference in the time it takes to pass through it; in other words, a pendulum will swing through a long arc just as quickly as through a short one. The reason that the long journey is made in the same time as the short one is this: the longer the arc the steeper are its ends, and on this account the *swifter* the pendulum will fall.

Does the time of one vibration depend upon the weight of the ball?—It is another curious property of the pendulum that whether it be made of lead or of wood or of other material, it will make its vibration in the same time. Its weight, and we may add, the material of which it is made, makes no difference in the time of one vibration.

Does the time of one vibration depend upon the size of the pendulum?—Nor does the size of the pendulum make any difference in the time of one vibration.

Of course the resistance of the air will be more on a large ball than on a small one, and on that account a large pendulum will not continue to vibrate as long as a small one, but they will swing from one end of the arc to the other in the same time, while the motion does continue, no matter how much they may differ in size.

Upon what does the time of one vibration depend?—But if we take pendulums of different lengths, as shown in Fig. 26, we shall find the longest one vibrating slowest. In all cases the longest pendulum needs the longest time to make one vibration. The time of one vibration depends altogether upon the length of the pendulum.

Fig. 26.

What is the law?—If the pendulum P (Fig. 26) is just *four* times as long as another, P', we shall find by trying the experiment that it takes just *twice* the time it does the other to make a vibration. We notice that:

The time of one vibration is in proportion to the square root of the length of the pendulum.

If then one pendulum is 9 times the length of another, it will take it 3 times as long to vibrate once.

The length of a pendulum that will vibrate in one second is about 39.1 inches: a pendulum $\frac{1}{4}$ of that length would vibrate in $\frac{1}{2}$ a second according to the law, since the square root of $\frac{1}{4}$ is $\frac{1}{2}$.

How is the pendulum used to measure time?—Now if we know the time it takes a pendulum to make one vibration, we may measure any length of time by simply counting the number made. The resistance of air would however soon stop the swinging, and, even if it did not, the counting of the vibrations would be a tedious task. Ingenious men have overcome these difficulties by inventing the clock, by which people are everywhere able to measure time.

Briefly describe its action.—In this instrument a weight or a spring keeps a set of wheels in motion, and these wheels keep the pendulum vibrating and at the same time register the number of vibrations it makes, by making an index or hand point to the divisions of a graduated circle.

Explain its action more fully.—In looking at the interior of a common clock, which is the best and perhaps the only way any one can clearly learn its action, we find that a pendulum is so connected with a toothed wheel that at the end of every two vibrations it allows one tooth to escape. If the pendulum vibrates twice a second it allows one tooth to escape at the end of each second, and if there are sixty teeth on the wheel it will turn around just once in sixty seconds or a minute. To the axis of this wheel the *second-hand* of the clock is fixed.

This wheel is connected with another that turns once around in an hour, and to the axis of this one the *minute-hand* is fastened.

There is still another wheel in the set which can turn once around in twelve hours, and to the axis of this the *hour-hand* is fastened.

How does a watch differ from a clock?—A watch differs from a clock in having a vibrating wheel, called the balance-wheel, instead of a pendulum. The vibration of the balance-wheel allows one tooth of a wheel to pass just as the pendulum does in the clock, and the number of beats is recorded in the same way.

What are chronometers?— Time-keepers of the most wonderful perfection have been made for the purpose of telling the longitude of a ship at sea, and for other purposes where great accuracy is required. They are called *chronometers.*

Concerning their perfect action Arnott says: After months spent in a passage from South America to Asia, my pocket chronometer, with others on board, announced one morning that a certain point of land was then bearing east from the ship at a distance of fifty miles; and in an hour afterwards, when a mist had cleared away, the looker-out on the mast gave the joyous call, " Land ahead," verifying the report of the chronometers almost to a mile after a voyage of thousands.

The method of using a watch to tell the longitude of a place on the earth may be found explained in astronomy.

What other use may be made of the pendulum?
—The pendulum has been used to determine the shape of the earth.

Describe the experiment with a vibrating cord.
—Let a small cord fastened at one end pass over two

Fig. 27.

bridges upon which it rests and be stretched by a heavy weight hung at the other end (Fig. 27). Then if a violin bow be drawn across the cord, or if a person, taking hold of its middle point, pull it aside and let it go again, it will swing back and forth so swiftly that its motions can not be connted, and it will look like a gauzy spindle, as the picture represents it.

What is meant by vibration and amplitude ?—The continued motion of the cord back and forth is called *vibration*. But when we speak of a vibration, or a single vibration, we mean *the motion from one side to the other and back again to the starting-point.*

The distance from one side to the other, that is, the distance through which any point of the cord travels, is called its *amplitude* of vibration.

Can the number of vibrations be counted ?—The motion of the cord is so very rapid that all we can see when it vibrates is a gauze-like swelling of its middle parts; and yet it is possible to find out exactly how many vibrations it makes in a second.

If the cord, like those of a violin or piano, gives a sound when it vibrates, the number of vibrations may be registered by the syren: for the number will be the same as the number of air-puffs which escape from that instrument when it makes a sound of the same pitch as that made by the cord, and the number of air-puffs is registered by the "hands" upon the upper part of the instrument, as seen in Fig. 31.

If the vibrations of the cord do not produce sound, yet the number made in one second may be very exactly shown by the aid of electricity. We will not attempt to describe the instrument now. See *Text-book of Philosophy*, p. 151.

Does the rapidity of vibration depend upon the length of the cord ?—When two cords are taken, one twice as long as the other, but alike in every other respect, it is found by experiment that the long one will vibrate only one half as fast as the other. In this case *the number of vibrations in a second is inversely as the length of the cord.*

This is also true of all other cases. If one string is, for example, one tenth as long as another, it will vibrate ten times as fast.

Does the rapidity of vibration depend upon the weight of the cord ?—The wire-wound string of a violin is much heavier than one which is not wound, and we find that it vibrates more slowly. The heavier the cord the slower the vibration. This is always true.

If, to be more particular, we take one cord four times as heavy as another, in all things else they being alike, it will vibrate only one half as fast. In all cases it will be true as it is in this one, that *the number of vibrations in a second is inversely as the square root of the weight of the cord.* If, for another example, we suppose one cord to weigh 16 times as much as another of the same length, it will vibrate only ¼ as fast.

What is the third thing on which the rapidity of vibration depends ?—The rapidity of vibration depends also on the weight or force by which the string is stretched. This weight or force is called the *tension* of the cord. If, for example, the weight which stretches the cord over the bridges in Fig. 27 is 56 lbs. the *tension* of the cord is said to be 56 lbs.

Now we find that, when other things are equal, the cord will vibrate faster as the tension is made greater. If the tensions of three cords are as the numbers 1, 4, 9, the number of vibrations a second will be as 1, 2, 3. But these last numbers are the square roots of the first, in their order, and this teaches us that *the number of vibrations a second is directly as the square root of the tension of the cord.*

To what are these principles applied?—In the manufacture of musical instruments in which the sounds are made by vibrating cords or wires, such as the guitar and the piano, these principles become important. The cords must each be of the right length and weight and tension, or else they will fail to give the correct tones for music.

Describe the vibration of a wire fixed at one end.—When a wire, or even a slender rod of wood, is fastened at one end in a vise, and its other end is drawn

Fig. 28.

aside, it will spring back and forth so swiftly as to appear
to be flattened out into a gauze-like fan (Fig. 28).

**On what does the rapidity of its vibration de-
pend?**—If the rod is shortened it will vibrate faster; in
a word, the number of vibrations in a second will depend
on the length of the wire or rod. The law seems to be
different from that which applies to cords. It states that
*the number of vibrations in a second is inversely as the
square of the length of the rod.* According to this law,
if one rod 36 inches long makes 1 vibration a second,

Fig. 29.

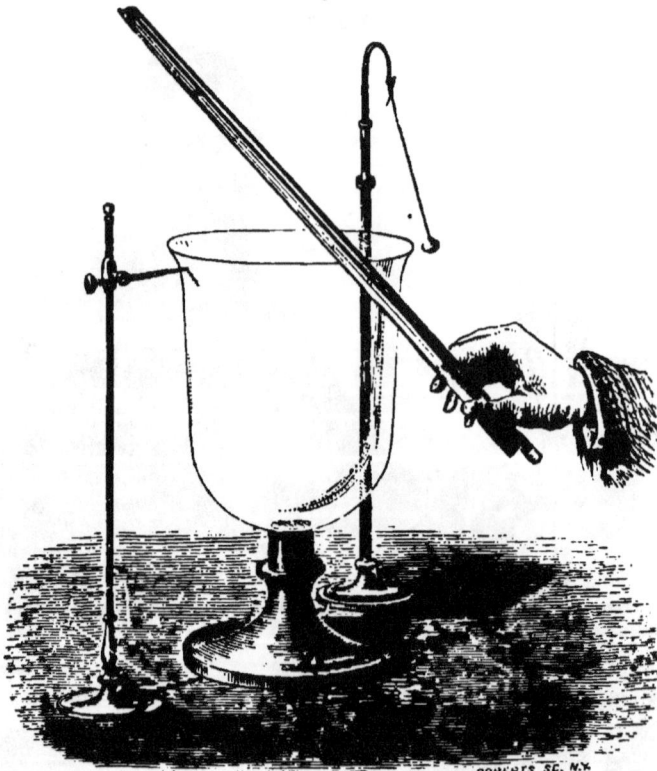

ROBERTS SC. N.Y.

another one only 12 inches long will make 9 in the same
time; being ⅓ as long it vibrates 9 times as fast.

How may the vibrations of a bell be shown?—
In Fig. 29 we are shown a bell-shaped glass vessel with a
little pendulum-ball hanging beside it. By drawing a
violin-bow across the edge of this bell we make the glass
vibrate, and we shall know that the vibrations are made
because the little pendulum-ball will fly back and forth
with a violent clatter. The edge of the glass, springing
back and forth, puts the ball in motion.

This is one of the many cases of vibration in which the
motion is too delicate to be seen, and the existence of
which would not be known if some way had not been
discovered by which to make the vibrations show themselves. Cases of such invisible vibrations are very common. In fact, almost every solid body we can see around

Fig. 30.

us is already or else may be put into a state of invisible
vibration.

How may the vibrations of a brass plate be shown?—If a plate of brass is fastened at its center, and a violin-bow be drawn across its edge (Fig. 30), it will vibrate. Its vibrations may be *felt* by gently touching it with the finger, but by sprinkling fine sand all over the plate its vibrations will be shown in a curious and much more satisfactory way. The picture represents the beautiful effect which will be produced. The sand will dance about, and finally collect into straight lines and curves, sometimes in one form and sometimes in another, changing with every change in the point to which the bow is applied or upon which the finger is laid. The reason for this curious arrangement is, that some parts of the plate vibrate more than others, and the sand gathers itself upon those points where there is the least motion.

How may the vibration of water be shown?—Let the glass vessel (Fig. 29) be almost filled with water, and the bow then drawn across its edge. The fluid will be thrown into violent commotion. Hosts of little wavelets will be thrown up and down in quick succession upon its surface, the water being thrown into vibration by the vibration of the glass.

By skillfully drawing the bow these wavelets may be brought into four and sometimes into six beautiful groups separated from each other by portions of water which seem to be at rest. Not many effects so fine can be so easily produced.

How may water-waves be made on a larger scale?—By tossing pebbles into the water of a quiet lake or pond we may cause circular waves which spread away farther and farther from the place where the pebble was dropped. By watching the motion of the water in these waves we may easily study the character of such vibrations.

In what direction does the water really move? —While looking at the growing circles of water started by the pebble it is most natural to think that the water is moving just as it appears to be—outward in all directions; and yet it is easy to show that it is not.

Little sticks and straws upon its surface would be carried along outward too, if such were the motion of the water, but we find that all the sticks and straws will do is simply to *rise* and *fall*, which shows that the real motion of the water is *up* and *down* only, and not outward from the pebble as it appears to be.

How is the motion in the billows of the sea?— The waves of the sea are of the same nature. The force of the wind, however, drives the water along at the same time that it is vibrating up and down. But the billows roll long after the wind has ceased to blow, and even they, at such times, are not able to carry along the bits of wood and other light bodies that may be floating upon them. Each wave will seem to roll out from under all such bodies, and let them down into the furrow to be lifted again by the next; and this shows that the real motion of the water is simply a motion up and down.

Does the air vibrate?—The air is so elastic that it yields to every force, even the very slightest, and then afterward springs back again. On this account it is in a state of vibration all the time. We can not stir a hand without causing the air to vibrate. It is made to tremble by every breath we exhale, and it quivers at every motion of our lips.

SOUND.

How is the sound of a piano-wire produced?—If we look carefully at a piano-wire while it is giving its sound we can often see that it is in motion; its appearance will be much like that shown in Fig. 27. And even if its delicate motions can not be *seen*, they may often be *felt* by placing the finger very gently upon the wire, or *heard* as a violent clatter if a knife-blade be used instead of the finger. The fact is that the sound of the wire is produced by these rapid vibrations.

Are other sounds produced in the same way?—By laying the finger gently upon the head of a drum a tremulous motion will be felt whenever the sound of the drum is heard. And in Fig. 29, while the motion of the little ball shows that the glass beside it is vibrating, a ringing sound is at the same time heard, and whenever a bell of any kind is ringing it may be shown that it is also vibrating. A body always vibrates when it emits a sound; all sounds are produced by vibrations.

Do all vibrations produce sound?—When a cord is long and not too tightly stretched (Fig. 27), its vibrations may be easily seen, but no sound will be heard.

A sudden motion of the hand puts the air in vibration, but gives no sound.

These and many other illustrations which might be given teach us that all vibrations do not produce sound.

What is the reason that some vibrations do not produce sound?—If we make the string, Fig. 27, vibrate *faster and faster*, by increasing the weight which stretches it, we shall very soon be able to hear a sound which it gives, and then if the weight be made less again the sound becomes inaudible. This shows that when the sound is not heard the vibrations of the cord are *too slow* to produce it. Some vibrations do not produce sound because they are too slow. The slowest vibrations that may produce sound are at the rate of 16 a second.

Is there another reason why vibrations do not produce sound?—A string or wire may be made so short and tense that its vibrations can not be heard. It then vibrates so very fast that no sound is made by its motion. Some vibrations are too fast to produce sound. The most rapid vibrations that can be heard are made at the rate of 38,000 a second.

What are sound-vibrations?—All vibrations between the limits of 16 a second and 38,000 a second may be called *sound-vibrations*. No others ought to be so called because, if any are either slower than 16 a second or swifter than 38,000 a second they can not be heard.

Is this true for all persons?—There are persons, however, to whose ears these limits will not apply. Some ears are more sensitive than others; they can hear sounds that others can not. The squeak of a bat is made by very rapid vibrations, and it is said that there are persons who can not hear it at all. The same thing may be said of the chirping of a cricket; two persons sitting in the presence of one of these animals may have ears of such different power that while one is annoyed by the shrillness of the cricket's voice, the other may not know that there is any noise produced. The limits named must, therefore, not be taken as absolute.

Will sound-vibrations pass through air ?—We could not hear the sound of a distant bell if the air did not bring its vibrations to our ears. But we may describe more carefully the way in which the sound comes to us. In the first place, the ringing bell is itself vibrating, as we know, and by these vibrations the air which is in contact with the metal is made to vibrate also. This air causes another portion beyond it to vibrate, and that in turn gives motion to another portion still farther away, until finally the air in contact with the ear is made to vibrate and then we hear the sound. Very quickly after the hammer strikes the bell, all the air between it and the ear is put in motion, but not until this motion has traveled, step by step, from the bell to the ear, can the sound be heard.

In this way all sounds made in the air travel from place to place. In speaking, our lips intrust their messages to the air and the air carries them to the ears of our friend and delivers them with the most perfect accuracy.

Will sound-vibrations pass through water ?—Let two stones be struck together under water and the sound of the blow will be distinctly heard above the surface. Or if the head is plunged beneath the surface while the blow is struck, the sound will be heard more distinctly than in air; its loudness will be likely to surprise the hearer. These things show that sound-vibrations pass through water with great facility.

Will sound-vibrations pass through solid bodies ? —To show that sound-vibrations also pass through wood, let the ear be placed upon one end of a long table while a pin is drawn across the other end. One who tries this experiment for the first time may be astonished to hear a sound so loud as the scratch of the pin will be. The sound-vibrations in this case travel through the wood of which the table is made.

The power of solids to convey sounds is also illustrated when boys at the station, waiting for a train of cars, put their ears upon the iron track to learn whether it is coming near. The sound of the train can be heard much farther through the solid iron than through the air.

"The American Indians understand that solid bodies, even the earth itself, convey sound with great facility. When these wild and artful people suspect that enemies are approaching they apply their ears close to the ground in order to discover the noises made by the footsteps of their foes when too far off for the sound to be conveyed through the air."

Can sound-vibrations pass through a vacuum?— We have seen that sounds can pass through solids, liquids, and gases, but we must remember that they can not pass unless one or another of these forms of matter is present.

This may be shown by experiment. A bell may be placed in the receiver of an air-pump, and be so fixed that while there it may be struck. Before the air is exhausted its ringing may be loud and clear, but long before the air is all taken out it will be almost too feeble to be heard at all. Sound can not pass through a vacuum.

What is the velocity of sound in different substances?—Sound travels faster in some substances than in others. By very careful experiments it has been found that in air whose temperature is 61° F, sound goes

4*

at the rate of 1,118 feet a second. It would travel faster through warmer air and more slowly in that which is colder.

In water, sound travels faster than in air; its velocity is about 4,714 feet a second.

In solid bodies the velocity of sound is still greater. In pine wood, for example, it travels at the rapid rate of 10,900 feet a second.

Do all kinds of sound go with the same velocity? —In air all sounds travel with the same rapidity. We may, for example, while listening to the music of a distant band, notice that the heavy sound of the drum and the shrill notes of the fife, made at the same moment, reach the ear together, and this shows that they must come with equal swiftness.

The same thing is true of all sounds whatever. Loud sounds and low sounds, the sweetest and the harshest alike, travel through the air at the rate of 1,118 feet a second. The overpowering roar of the thunder can not outrun the delicate song of the sparrow. In any medium all sounds travel with equal velocity.

How can we measure distances by sound? —If sound goes through air at the rate of 1,118 feet each second, it will go twice that distance in two seconds and ten times that distance in ten seconds; so that we need only to multiply 1,118 feet by the number of seconds to tell how far the sound has come.

A man is chopping wood in the distance, and you wish to know how far he is away: watch the motions of his axe and listen to the sound of the blows. You will hear the sound while the axe is over his head. The sound is made when the blow is struck, and it takes as long for the sound to come to you as it does for the axe to be lifted.

If it is one second between the time you see the blow and the time you hear the sound, then the woodman must be 1,118 feet away.

Give another example.—In a similar way you may tell how far off a flash of lightning occurs. The sound of thunder is made when the lightning is seen, but it is not often heard until several moments afterward. If you can count the seconds between the flash and the roar you may multiply 1,118 feet by the number, and this will give the number of feet to the place where the lightning occurred.

Upon what does the loudness of sound depend ?—The harder one strikes a piano-key the louder the sound of the note will be, but all that the heavier blow does is to make the piano-wire vibrate through greater distances. In all cases the loudest sounds are caused by vibrations through the greatest distances.

Now the distance through which the vibrating particles swing back and forth is called the *amplitude* of vibration, and hence we may say that the loudness of sound depends upon the *amplitude* of the vibrations which produce it.

The harder one strikes a bell the louder it rings, because the heavier blow causes the particles of the bell to vibrate through greater distances, or, in other words, to have a greater amplitude of vibration.

What effect does distance have upon the loudness of sound ?—The deafening roar of a cataract when heard through a distance of several miles becomes a gentle murmur, and the deep-toned thunder, if made too far away, can not be heard at all.

A powerful human voice may be heard at a distance of about 700 feet; at greater than that distance it is generally too feeble to be heard.

Sounds, however loud when near at hand, die away in the distance until they become inaudible.

Why is this?—This is because the amplitude of the vibrations of the air grows less and less as the distance is greater and greater, until at last it is too little to affect the ear.

How can we illustrate this?—When a pebble is dropped into quiet water, the height of the circling waves is greatest near the center where the pebble is dropped, and grows less and less as they spread outward, until at last we can not see the waves at all. So when a bell is struck, the amplitude of the air-waves near to the bell is greatest, and it grows less and less as the waves spread outward in all directions from the bell, until at last it is so little that the sound can not be heard.

Which will convey sound farthest, solids, liquids, or gases?—In solid bodies the vibrations diminish slowly, and on this account sounds may be heard through them at long distances. In liquids the vibrations diminish more rapidly than in solids, so that through them sounds can not be heard as far. In gases the vibrations die out still faster, and hence sounds can not be heard as far in them as in either of the other forms of matter.

We now see why the sound of a coming train of cars can be heard sooner by placing the ear to the iron track. The solid iron conveys the sound to the station, but in the air the vibrations die away before they get there.

Can sound be heard farther in air at some times than at others?—When the air is dense, as in a cold still winter morning, or damp, as it often is in a still June evening, we all know how much more distinctly distant sounds can be heard than at other times. The rattling of carriages, the laughing of children, the songs of birds, and a thousand other sounds, many of which at other times would not be noticed, are heard with surprising clearness in still damp summer evenings.

What is the law ?—But whether a sound can be heard through a distance great or small, the rapidity with which it dies away is governed by the following law:

The intensity or loudness of sound is inversely as the square of the distance from its source.

We understand by this law that at twice the distance sound will be only one fourth as loud; or at one half the distance it will be four times as loud.

Will a tube convey sound ?—If we put our lips to one end of a long tube of metal, or even of pasteboard, while a friend puts his ear at the other end, we find that even a gentle whisper will be very distinctly heard.

A gentleman in the city of Paris tried the experiment with one of the water-pipes of that city, and found that a word spoken in a very low tone was heard by a friend three fourths of a mile away, while, as we have already learned, a powerful voice in the free air would not be heard more than one fifth of that distance.

Why can sounds be heard farther in tubes ?—The reason that sounds can be heard so much farther in tubes than in free air is that the tube keeps the vibrations from spreading in all directions outward as they do in the atmosphere. They are all collected in the tube and sent forward together, and they will not die away as fast as when allowed to scatter in all directions in the air.

What are such tubes called ?—Such tubes are called *speaking tubes*. They are often placed in dwellings so that the mistress may talk with her servants even while they are in different and distant rooms. They are also placed

in large hotels for a similar purpose, and in large manu-
facturing establishments they are very common and a
great convenience.

What is an echo?—Who, after loudly uttering some
word or sentence, has not at some time heard the sound of
his voice coming back to him from a distant wood, or
perhaps from the wall of a distant building? A part of
the last word spoken, if not the whole of it, and sometimes
more words than the last one, may be heard as distinctly
as if some mimic were shouting back what he had heard.
Such sounds are called echoes.

How is an echo produced?—When we throw a ball
perpendicularly against the floor it bounds directly back
to the hand. In the same way when the sound of our
voice strikes perpendicularly against a distant wall, it
bounds back to us and we catch it in our ears, and thus
hear the word which we uttered, as an echo.

Or, if we throw a ball obliquely against the floor it
bounds away obliquely from us: we can not catch it, but
it may be caught by another person standing in the right
place. In much the same way if a sound strikes obliquely
against a distant wall it will be thrown obliquely away
from it, and a person standing in its path will hear the
sound as if it came to him obliquely from the wall. It
is in this way that we hear the echoes of sounds which are
not made by ourselves.

What is reflection of sound?—When sound is
thrown back from a surface against which it strikes, it is
said to be *reflected*.

Mention some remarkable echoes.—An echo in
Woodstock Park repeats seventeen syllables distinctly.
Another near Milan repeats a single syllable thirty times:

in this case the sound is thrown from one reflecting surface to another many times, and each reflection sends an
echo to the hearer.

"Placing himself close to the upper part of the wall of
the London Coliseum, a circular building 130 feet in
diameter, Mr. Wheatstone found a word pronounced to
be repeated a great many times. A single exclamation
sounded like a peal of laughter, while the tearing of a
piece of paper was like the patter of hail."

MUSICAL SOUNDS.

What was Galileo's experiment?—Galileo passed
the back of his knife-blade quickly over the rough edge of
a coin and produced a musical sound. You may repeat his
experiment easily, or in the absence of a coin with ridges
upon its edge, you may use a piece of one of the heavier
strings of a violin or piano, which are wound with fine
wire; or, indeed, if there is nothing better at hand, the
edge of a small file may be used. If you pass the blade
slowly over one of these rough surfaces a series of unpleas-
ant taps will be heard, but pass it swiftly and you will
produce a shrill musical sound.

How may a note be produced by a slate-pencil?
—"Every schoolboy knows how to produce a note with
his slate-pencil. Holding it vertically and somewhat
loosely between the fingers, on moving it over the slate
a succession of taps is heard. By pressure these taps can
be caused to follow each other so quickly as to produce a
continuous sound. We must not call it musical, because
this term is associated with pleasure, and the sound of the
pencil is not pleasant." But it is a *continuous* tone, and
yet we know that it is made up of separate taps of the
pencil.

May other separate sounds be made to cause a musical sound?—Any sound whatever, repeated fast enough, will produce a continuous sound or a tone. To illustrate this curious fact still further, suppose a stiff card is held against the edge of a cog-wheel turning slowly; the card will strike each cog that comes around and every blow will be heard separately, but when the wheel turns swiftly the same blows, made faster, produce a continuous and shrill musical sound.

If a watch could tick fast enough, say 80 or 100 times a second, no one would be able to count the ticks, or even to hear them separately, for they would produce a steady musical sound.

Could the blows of a hammer upon an anvil be made fast enough and with regularity, they would produce a clear and powerful musical tone.

Fig. 81.

Even puffs of air when made in quick succession result in music. This interesting fact is shown by means of the siren—a very ingenious instrument which we must now describe.

Describe the siren.—In Fig. 31 this instrument is represented. A pipe, P, enters a wind-chest, W. The top of this chest is pierced with a circular row of holes. A disk of metal lies very near to the top of the wind-chest and is pierced with holes exactly corresponding with those in the chest itself. The disk is so fixed that it may be made to revolve very swiftly, and the pointers, like the hands of a clock, seen at the top of the picture, are to tell the number of turns the disk makes in a second.

Now suppose the holes in the disk are exactly over those in the top of the chest. Then if a blast of air is forced through the pipe, P, into the chest, it can escape through the holes in steady streams; but let the disk be turned just a little so that its holes are not directly over the others: by this means the holes in the chest will be closed so that the streams of air can not escape. As the disk revolves the holes in the chest will be rapidly opened and shut, and the streams of air will, in this way, be cut up into puffs.

When the disk turns slowly the separate puffs may be heard, but when it goes rapidly these same puffs produce a musical tone of great purity.

What is necessary, then, to produce a musical sound ?—All that seems necessary to produce a musical tone out of any sound whatever is that the separate pulses be made with sufficient regularity and swiftness.

What is meant by the pitch of musical sounds ?— To distinguish musical sounds as being high or low, the term *pitch* is used.

Some sounds, like the gravest notes of an organ, are so very low that we can scarcely hear them, while others, like the highest notes of the piano, are so very high that they are very far above the reach of any human voice. Between the highest and the lowest there may be a multitude of musical notes whose only difference is a difference in *pitch*.

Upon what does pitch depend ?—If we take several strings all alike, except in length, we shall find that the shortest string always gives the highest sound. And now if we remember that the shortest string always vibrates the fastest, we see that the highest tone is the one that is made by the most rapid vibrations.

This is true in all cases. The pitch of musical sound depends entirely upon the rapidity of vibration.

Upon what does the rate of vibration of a string depend ?—The rapidity of vibration of a string or wire, as we learned while studying the subject (p. 71). depends upon the *length* of the string, its *tension*, and its *weight*.

How then may we vary the pitch of the sounds of strings ?—If we change either the length of the vibrating string, or its tension, or its weight, we change the pitch of the sound it produces.

To shorten the string makes the tone higher; to increase the tension also makes the tone higher; but to increase the weight of the string makes the tone lower.

How is the pitch of the sounds obtained in the piano ?—In the piano the sounds are made by the vibration of wires. These wires are of different lengths and also of different weights; the shortest and the lightest giving the highest tone. Now one end of each wire is wound around a screw, and by turning the screw in one direction the wire is tightened and the pitch raised, but by turning it the other way the wire is loosened and the pitch lowered.

How is the pitch obtained in a violin ?—The violin has four strings, each having a weight different from the others, the lightest string giving the highest note. Each string is wound upon a "key" by which it may be tightened or slackened, the tighter string giving the higher note. They are all of the same length, but the player changes the length of the vibrating part of each at pleasure by pressing a finger upon it at any desired point.

By having the right difference in the weight, the tension, and the length of the strings, the correct pitch of the notes is obtained.

How is the sound of the organ produced ?—In the organ the musical sounds are caused by vibrations of columns of air. A large bellows is kept full of air; the organist, by pressing the keys of the organ, opens the way from this bellows into one or more of the many pipes of the instrument, and jets of air going into the pipes at the bottom, make the air throughout their whole lengths vibrate, and these vibrations produce the musical sounds.

Upon what does the pitch of organ-tones depend ?—The pitch of the tone in an organ depends on the length of the organ-pipe. The shorter the pipe the higher the pitch will be.

The lowest note used in music is made by an organ-pipe, open at the top, whose length is 32 feet. If the pipe is closed at the top, a note of the same pitch will be made by a pipe 16 feet in length. The highest notes are made by pipes which are only a few inches long.

LIGHT.

What are luminous bodies?—Luminous bodies are those which produce light. The sun is a luminous body because it shines by light which itself produces. The flame of a candle, and a red-hot iron ball, are also luminous bodies for the same reason.

What are non-luminous bodies?—Non-luminous bodies are those that do not produce light. If they shine at all it is because they first receive light from some other source and then throw it off again. A piece of rock or of wood, a flower, a cloud,—all these are non-luminous bodies. The moon is also non-luminous, for while it shines with a steady and bright light, yet it produces none itself. What we call the moonlight is light which goes from the sun to the moon first, and is then thrown from the moon to us.

What are transparent and opaque bodies?—Some bodies, like glass and air, allow light to pass freely through them; all such are called *transparent* bodies. Others, like iron and wood, forbid the passage of light through them; such are called *opaque* bodies.

Is any substance perfectly transparent?—We do not mean that a transparent body will allow *all* the light that falls upon it to go through. The air, for example, which is one of the most transparent of all things, does not let all the sunlight come through it. One can often look directly at the sun, rising in the morning or setting in the evening, without doing any injury to the eye, but if the air did not shut out a large portion of the sun's light a single glance would blind him. Perhaps no substance exists which is *perfectly* transparent.

Is any substance perfectly opaque?—On the other hand, small quantities of light will pass through wood and even through gold, for we all know that it is easy to see through a thin shaving of almost any kind of wood, and, if a piece of gold-leaf is at hand, we may hold it between the eye and a window and see that light comes through it: this light is green.

What are rays, beams, and pencils of light?—A *ray* is a single line of light. Several parallel rays together form a *beam* of light.

The ray of light is quite too delicate a thing to be obtained in practice; the smallest line of light which it is possible to use is made of many rays; it is a beam.

A *pencil* of light is a collection of rays that are not parallel.

In what direction does light go from a luminous body?—If a lamp is suddenly lighted in the center of a dark room, every part of the room will be instantly made light. This shows that the light goes from the flame in all directions. In the same way light is given from a glowing coal, from a red-hot iron, from the sun, indeed, from all luminous bodies, in every possible direction at once.

Does it move in straight lines?—In order to show by experiment whether the path of light is straight or crooked we need a darkened room. It is, easy to darken a room by closing the shutters, and at the same time, if need be, hanging shawls or blankets over the windows. If a small hole is made in one of the shutters to let the sunlight through, the path of the sunbeam in the room may be distinctly seen. If the air is sprinkled with chalk-dust the beam is peculiarly bright and beautiful, and no artist could possibly draw a line so absolutely straight as it is seen to be.

We often see such beams coming through our half closed window-shutters and streaking the dusty air of our rooms with bars of light,— beautiful illustrations of the fact that light always moves in straight lines.

What other illustrations of this fact ?—When the sun is sinking behind clouds in the western sky, it often presents an appearance which is very well shown in the picture (Fig. 32), and which is sometimes described by saying that the sun "draws water." Is it possible that any one ever believed the streaks he saw were really streams of water being pulled up by the sun? We know now that they are beams of light from the sun, which is shining through openings in the clouds. They are made in just the same way as are the beams of light seen in our rooms when the sun shines through openings in the win-dow-shutter.

How are shadows made?—It is upon the same principle that shadows are made. To illustrate, just put a book at a convenient distance in front of a lamp-flame. Now some of the rays of light fall upon the book, and can not go farther, but others just graze the edges of the book and pass in *straight lines* onward, so that behind the book and reaching to the opposite wall is a space from which the light is shut out. *This space which is deprived of light is the shadow* of the book.

We are apt to call the black spot on the wall the shadow,

but the shadow really reaches from the book to the wall; it is all the space behind the book from which the light is shut out, and the black spot on the wall is only one end of it.

Fig. 32.

Of what two parts is a shadow composed?—If we examine the end of the true shadow of the book as it appears upon the wall, we may notice that there is a dark middle part, and then a border all around this, which is much lighter. One can hardly fail to see these two parts by examining the shadows made by objects around the evening lamp. There is in every shadow a dark middle part surrounded by another lighter portion. The dark middle part is called the *umbra*, and the lighter portion is called the *penumbra*. These parts reach throughout the whole length of every shadow.

How are they formed?—A very easy experiment will explain how these two parts of a shadow are produced. Place two lamp-flames on a table near each other, and hold a lead pencil or a narrow strip of wood between the flames and a sheet of paper, at some distance from them. Two distinct shadows will be seen, one cast by each light. Now move the pencil nearer to the paper, the shadows will approach each other, until at last they overlap and form one, in which the umbra and the penumbra may be seen with surprising clearness. The umbra gets no light from either flame, but it is easy to see that every part of the penumbra is getting light from one or the other. On this account the umbra is darker than the penumbra.

Is it so with a single flame?—Now in the shadow cast when a single flame is used, the outer parts are getting light from *one edge or another of the flame*, while the middle part is getting no light at all from any portion of the flame. For this reason the umbra is darker than the penumbra.

What is the velocity of light?—The light from the flash of a gun in the distance comes to us so very quickly that it is impossible to measure the brief time it takes. So swiftly does light travel, that, could it move in curved lines, it would go around the world more than seven times in a second! Its rate of motion or velocity is about 190,000 miles a second.

It will, of course, be interesting to know how a velocity so very great could be measured. It was first done by the Danish astronomer, Römer, about two hundred years ago.

How was the velocity of light found?—This gentleman, by observing the eclipse of one of Jupiter's satellites, found out how long it takes light to go across the orbit of the earth, and he then divided that distance by the number of seconds, and so found out how far the light could go in one second.

Explain the operation more fully.—The time when an eclipse of Jupit r's moon is to begin is exactly known, as it would be seen when the earth is in that part of its orbit which is nearest to Jupiter. Now if the earth is in the opposite part of the orbit, the eclipse will not be seen to begin at the moment at which it is predicted, but 16 minutes and 36 seconds, or 996 seconds afterward. It is seen by light which comes from it, and the reason it begins late is that the light has so much farther to come. In fact it takes the light 996 seconds to go across the orbit of the earth. The distance across is about 190,000,000 miles, and 190 millions divided by 996 gives about 190,000 for the number of miles that light can travel in one second of time.

How does distance affect the intensity of light?
—The nearer a body is to the source of light, the brighter or more intense will be the light that falls upon it.

Let us study this subject more closely by experiment. We may take a sheet of paper, or, what is a little better, a square of stiff card-board, and hold it half way between a lamp-flame and the wall of a room. If we measure the shadow on the wall, we find it to be just twice as long and twice as wide as the card-board, and hence its surface is just four times as large as that of the board.

Now if the light that falls upon the card-board could go to the wall it would cover the whole surface of the shadow, and be spread over a surface four times as large as that on which it does fall. Being spread over four times as much surface it can be only one fourth as bright.

5

We see from this experiment that at 2 times the distance from the flame the light is only one quarter as intense. If the distance is taken 3 instead of 2, the intensity would be only one ninth. The law is this:

The intensity of light varies inversely as the square of the distance from its source.

The light of the stars is dim, but if any one of these glimmering points could be brought as near to us as the sun, it would be more dazzling than that body is to us. Or, if the sun could be carried out as far as the stars, it would be no brighter than they.

How can we see objects?—A luminous body is seen by means of light which comes directly from it into our eyes. It is the light which *comes from* a red-hot iron ball which enables us to see it.

We see non-luminous bodies also by means of light which comes from them: it is impossible to see any object that does not send light into the eye.

How can this be true of non-luminous bodies?—Non-luminous bodies have no light of their own to send to the eye, but they receive light from luminous bodies, and throw it off again into the air. This light which they throw off may enter our eyes, and by this means the body becomes visible.

All non-luminous bodies are invisible in a very cloudy night, because no light from the sun or moon or stars falls upon them, and they can send none to the eye. All objects in our room disappear instantly when the lamp is extinguished, because no light then falls upon them, and we therefore get none from them.

What is reflected light?—This light which is thrown off from non-luminous bodies is called *reflected* light.

What experiment can illustrate reflection of light ?—Let a beam of sunlight into a darkened room through a hole A, Fig. 33, in the shutter of a window, and make it fall upon a looking-glass. This beam will bound off, or be reflected from the glass, and go up to the ceiling, where it will form a bright spot C. Let the air of the room be sprinkled with dust, and the beams of light will

Fig. 33.

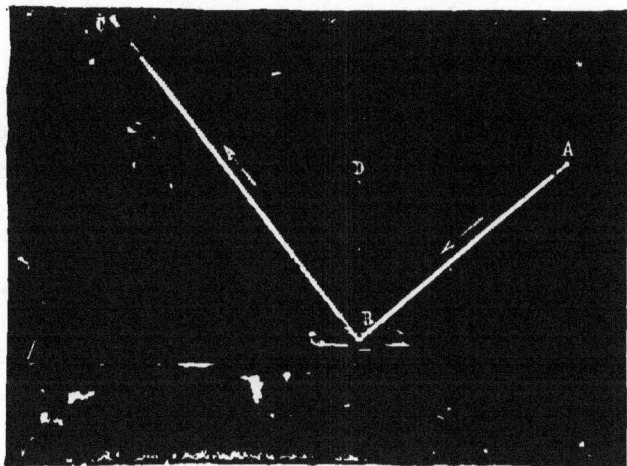

be shown as clearly as they are represented in the picture, which is a very good picture of the experiment.

What are important parts to notice here ?—It is very necessary to understand clearly the use of certain terms which are applied to certain things represented in this figure. There is first the beam AB, which *falls upon the reflecting surface*, and is called the *incident beam ;* and then the beam BC, which is *thrown from the reflecting surface*, and is called the *reflected beam.* The point B is called the *point of incidence.*

And now, if we suppose a perpendicular BD to be

erected, we have two angles made, one, ABD, the angle between the incident beam and the perpendicular, is the *angle of incidence ;* the other, CBD, the angle between the reflected beam and the perpendicular, is the *angle of reflection.*

What is the law of reflection?—Now these two angles are exactly equal in this experiment: they are always so. The law of reflection states that the angle of reflection must be equal to the angle of incidence.

What are mirrors?—Some bodies reflect light much better than others. Very little is reflected from the surface of rough iron, for example, while a great deal is thrown from the surface of new tin. Those which reflect light most freely are called *mirrors.*

A common looking-glass is the most familiar example of a mirror, but other forms are almost as common. The inside surface of a bright silver spoon is a good mirror, and the outside surface also, because from both these surfaces light is very freely reflected.

What are three forms of mirror?—There are three forms of mirrors which need especial notice:

First, the *plane* mirror, one whose surface is like that of the looking-glass, plane or flat.

Second, the *concave* mirror, one whose surface is like that of the inside of the silver spoon, hollowed or concave.

Third, the *convex* mirror, one whose surface is like the outside of the silver spoon, rounded or convex.

What effect do plane mirrors cause?—If light from any object falls upon a plane mirror, and after reflection enters our eyes, we see an image of the object (Fig. 34). It appears to be behind the mirror, and just as far behind it as the object itself is in front (Fig. 35).

Fig. 34.

Give examples.—Our own image seen in a looking-glass is the most familiar example of this effect, but looking down into the water of a well or of a lake will show the image just as perfectly. The surface of quiet water is indeed a very perfect plane mirror, and forms images of all objects above it with wonderful clearness. How beautiful are the pictures of the mansions and shrubbery along the bank of a river, or near the shores of a lake, as we see them presented in the still water between us and them!

How are images formed?—The way in which this

curious effect is produced may be understood by studying Fig. 35, which represents a boy looking at the image of a candle in a looking-glass.

Fig. 85.

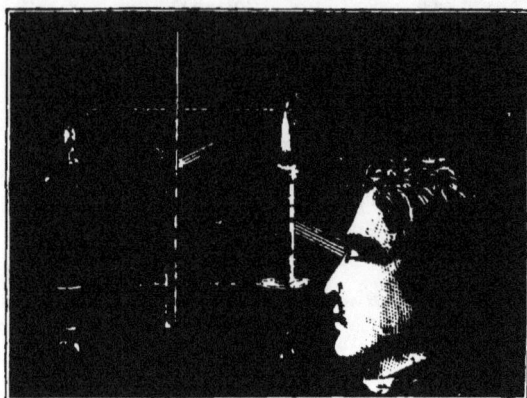

Rays of light are shown going from the tip of the candle-flame to the mirror, and being reflected from it into the eye of the boy. These rays *appear* to have come from a point *behind* the mirror, and this point is the image of the tip of the flame from which the rays first started.

Now every point on the whole candle will send rays to the mirror to be thrown back into the same eye, and thus form an image of every point, or in other words an image of the candle itself.

And so, when a person sees his own image in a mirror, he may think of its being formed in the same way. He may think of rays of light going from *every point* on his person to the mirror, and thence, being reflected, coming into his eyes, and then he may think of his eyes tracing these rays right back, in the direction from which they last came, to points behind the mirror; these points make up the image which he sees.

How may more than one image of an object be made at once?—By using two looking-glasses several images of one object may be seen at once.

By placing two looking-glasses parallel to each other and near together, and then putting the eye at one end, while a ball or other object is put between them at the other, a large number of images of the ball may be seen. The picture, Fig. 36, shows how the light must be reflected

Fig. 36.

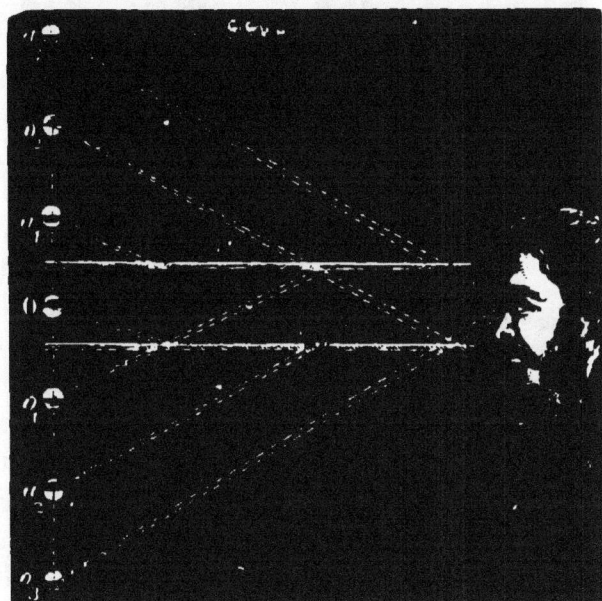

back and forth from one mirror to the other to make so many images.

How may just three be formed?—By holding two mirrors at right angles (Fig. 37), any object placed between them will give three images.

Fig. 37.

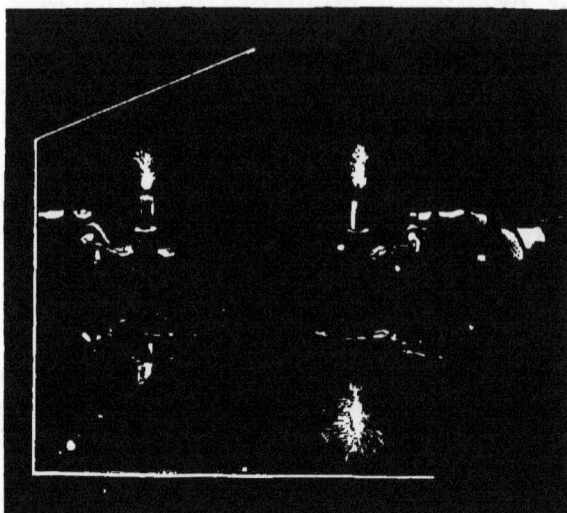

How may five be obtained ?—But if instead of being at right angles the mirrors are inclined, as in Fig. 38, making an angle of 60°, just five images will be formed.

Fig. 38.

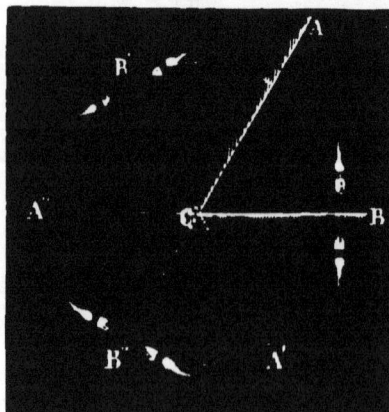

What is the effect of a concave mirror upon a beam of light ?—Fig. 39 shows the effect of a concave mirror on parallel rays. The rays, after reflection, will no longer be parallel; they will converge and cross each other at the point F.

This point is called the *focus* of the mirror. Any point where rays, after reflection, cross each other, is a focus; but when the mirror is held perpendicular to the path of the beam, as in the picture, the focus is called the *principal focus.*

What is the effect of the concave mirror on diverging rays?—Let a candle-flame be held some distance

Fig. 89.

before a concave mirror (Fig. 40), and the light reflected will make a bright spot upon the finger or any thing else

Fig. 40.

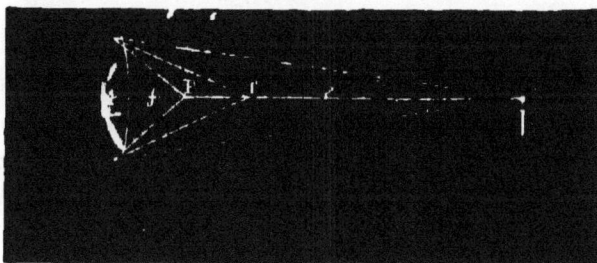

held at the point F. We see that while the rays from the candle are diverging, those which are thrown from the mirror are converging.

What effect does a concave mirror always produce?—In both these pictures we notice that the rays, after reflection, are brought nearer together than they were before, or, in other words, that they are *collected* by reflection. A concave mirror always makes the rays go on nearer together after reflection than they did before.

5*

Describe the image formed by a concave mirror when an object is placed very near.—By holding one of these instruments very near to the face, a person can hardly recognize himself in the immense image which he sees. The picture (Fig. 41) represents a concave mirror, M, with a young man standing very near to it; his

Fig. 41.

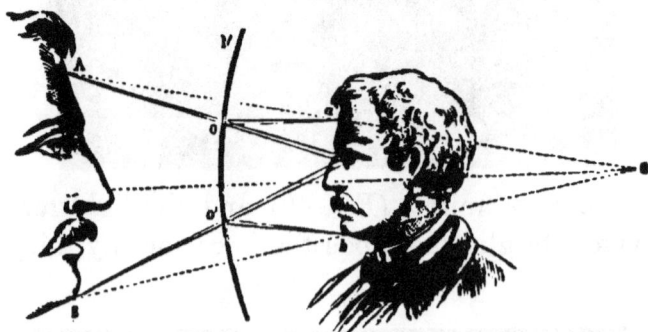

face is supposed to be between the focus and the mirror. The image formed is much larger than the object, and seems to be almost upon the surface of the mirror, instead of being as far behind it as we are accustomed to see it in a common looking-glass.

The concave mirror always forms an image larger than the object if the object is very near to it.

Suppose the object is moved away from the mirror?—If a candle is put a little farther away from the mirror than the focus, a still more curious effect will be produced. The image will not appear behind the mirror at all; it will be in front of it and farther away than the object itself, and, curiously enough, always bottom upward, or inverted.

The picture (Fig. 42) represents the experiment. The

image could not be seen if a screen were not put in just
the right place to receive it, because no light would come

Fig. 42.

from it to our eyes. The screen receives the light which
forms the image and reflects it to the eye.

Now let the object be moved still farther away.
—If the candle is carried still farther away from the
mirror, the image will move up toward it and grow smaller.
At length the object and the image will be at equal distances from the mirror; they will then be of equal size,
but as the candle is carried out farther and farther the
image will go nearer and nearer to the mirror, growing
smaller and smaller all the time, until finally it appears
only as a bright spot at the focus.

The concave mirror is the only form that can produce images in front of it, or that are inverted.

Describe the image by a convex mirror.—Fig. 43 shows the small image which is formed when a person

Fig. 43.

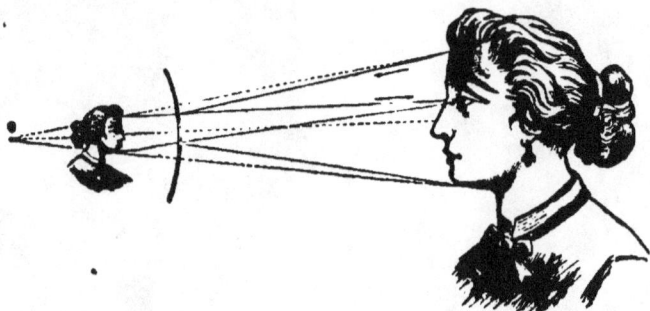

looks into a convex mirror. It is always, as we see it here represented, behind the surface of the mirror, erect, and smaller than the object.

Fig. 44.

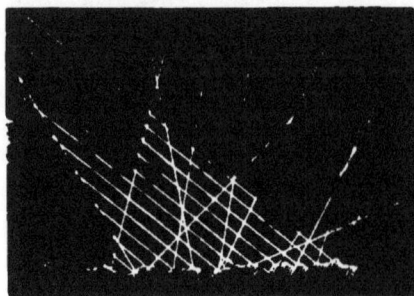

How is light reflected from rough surfaces? —When a beam of light falls upon a rough sur- face it is reflected irregu- larly. This effect is shown in Fig. 44. The result is that the reflected light is scattered in every di- rection.

Do the rays obey the law of reflection?—When we say that the reflection is irregular, we do not mean that the rays are not thrown off according to the law of reflection. That law is never transgressed. Every ray must be thrown in such a direction that the angle of reflection is equal to the angle of incidence. But on a rough surface, like that seen in Fig. 44, the reflecting points are not in regular order, and for this reason the reflected rays are not.

Do transparent bodies reflect light?—Transparent bodies do reflect light: we know this from the simple fact that we are able to see them; for we have learned before, that an object is visible only by the light which is thrown from it into our eyes. Glass and water are transparent bodies, and yet these bodies are able to reflect a great deal of light.

How do they differ from opaque bodies?—An opaque body does not allow light to pass through it; a transparent body allows the light to pass through it freely. For instance, we can not look through a piece of sheet-iron; it stops the light and reflects it, but we see distinctly through glass, because it can reflect only a part of all the light that falls upon it and allows the rest to come through.

Can this be shown by experiment?—Water is as transparent as glass, and we can easily show that water does not reflect all the light that falls upon its surface. The picture (Fig. 45) tells us at once how such an experiment is to be made. A glass vessel filled with water is placed so that a beam of sunlight coming into a dark room through a hole in a shutter can fall upon the surface of the fluid. The beam of light *can be seen* in its passage through the water.

All transparent bodies allow light to go through them in this way, but it is not always possible to see the path of the rays.

Fig. 45.

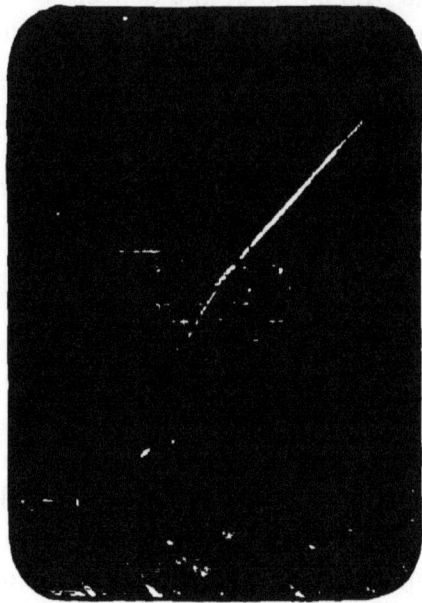

What else may be noticed in the experiment?—
If the air in the room is a little dusty, the path of light
from the window to the water, as well as through the
water itself, can be seen, and then it will be noticed that
the beam seems to be *broken* just at the point where it
enters the liquid.   This is also shown in the picture.
The beam is perfectly straight while in the air, and perfectly straight while in the water also, but it is bent just
where it passes from one into the other.

Is this always the case ?—This bending of the rays
of light in passing from one transparent substance into
another generally takes place.

The light that comes through the windows into our
houses is bent twice, once when it passes from the air

outside into the glass, and again when it passes from the glass into the air in the room.

What is this bending of the rays called?—This bending of the rays of light in passing from one substance into another is called *refraction*.

What terms must now be understood?—To explain certain terms used in connection with the subject of refraction we must first suppose a line to be drawn perpendicular to the surface where refraction occurs, and to be extended both ways from it, or into both substances. In Fig. 46, for instance, we must suppose a line perpendicular to the water at the point I, where the light R I enters, and to reach up into the air and down into the water. Then we have,

Fig. 46.

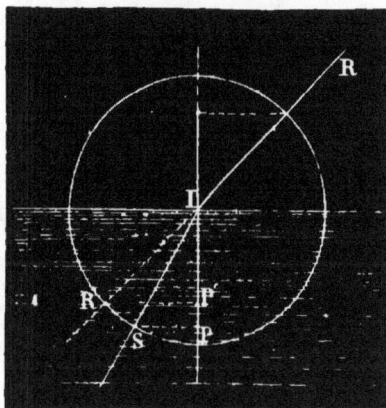

The *incident beam*—that which falls upon the substance into which it is to pass, R I:

The *refracted beam*—that which passes through the second substance, I S:

The *angle of incidence*—the angle between the incident beam and the perpendicular:

The *angle of refraction*—the angle between the refracted beam and the perpendicular.

On what does the amount of refraction depend? —Some substances bend the rays more than others. The amount of bending depends upon the difference in the density of the two substances. If two substances could have exactly the same density, light would pass from one to the other without being bent at all; but if one is more dense than the other, the bending will occur. For instance, water is more dense than air, so that light which passes either from air into water or from water into air, will be refracted.

What is the law of refraction?—If the rays are passing from one medium into a denser one the angle of refraction will be smaller than the angle of incidence, but if passing into one which is less dense the angle of refraction will be larger than the angle of incidence.

If, for illustration, the beam R I (Fig. 46) is the incident beam going from air down into water, it will be bent so as to go in the direction I S. Now it is easy to see that the angle S I P, in the water, or the angle of refraction, is smaller than the angle in the air, or the angle of incidence.

But suppose S I represents a beam going from the water up into the air above, it will be bent so as to go in the direction of I R. In this case the angle in the air is the angle of refraction: the angle of incidence is in the water. The light is passing into a less dense substance and the angle of refraction is larger than the angle of incidence.

How does a straight stick appear when partly plunged into water?—If a straight stick is plunged a part of its length into clear water it will look as if it were broken or bent just at the surface of the water. This effect is caused by refraction, and it is very common. Boatmen are especially familiar with it, since their oars always look bent at the point where they enter the water. (Fig. 47.)

Why does the stick appear to be bent?—Of course the oar or stick is not bent, and it looks to be so only because the light that *comes out of the water from it* is bent

Fig. 47.

when it enters the air, and the part that is in the water
will appear to be in the direction in which the light from
it enters the eye. All this may be understood if you
carefully examine Fig. 48, where the true place of the

Fig. 48.

stick in water is shown
by dotted lines, and two
rays that come from
the lower end of it are
shown bent at the sur-
face of the water, so
as to enter the eye,
which traces them back
in *straight lines*, so that
they seem to come from
a point above the one
from which they started.

What is another curious effect of refraction?—
Water does not appear to be as deep as it really is on
account of the refraction of the light which comes from
the bottom into the air. The young man represented in
Fig. 50 sees the bottom of the water lifted far toward the
surface. The rays of light from the point O, for example,
are refracted at the surface

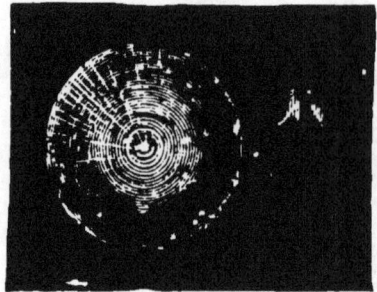

Fig. 49.

and by this means enter
the eye as if they came
from O′; and so the bot-
tom at O seems to be
at O′.

What are lenses?—
The instruments used to
refract light are called len-
ses; they are transparent bodies having either one or two
curved surfaces.

Fig. 49 is a picture of one kind of lens. Looking at
the side of the instrument it is circular; looking at the
edge of it, it is found to be thicker through the middle;
both sides are convex. This is called the *double convex*
lens.

Sometimes both sides of the lens are concave and the
middle is thinner than the edge ; in this case it is called a
double concave lens.

How many kinds are there ?—There are six different forms of lens. They are shown in section by Fig. 51.
They are named as follows :

1 The double convex.	4 The double concave.
2 " plano convex.	5 " plano concave.
3 " meniscus.	6 " concavo convex.

The first three act upon light in the same way : on

Fig. 50.

this account only the first or double convex lens will be particularly noticed.

Fig. 51.

The last three are alike also in their effect, and we need give close attention only to the action of the double concave.

What is the effect of the convex lens on parallel

rays ?—If a double convex lens is held in the path of a sunbeam, especially in a darkened room, the rays will not come out of it parallel: they will be so bent as to all come to one point, as we are shown by Fig. 52.

Fig. 52.

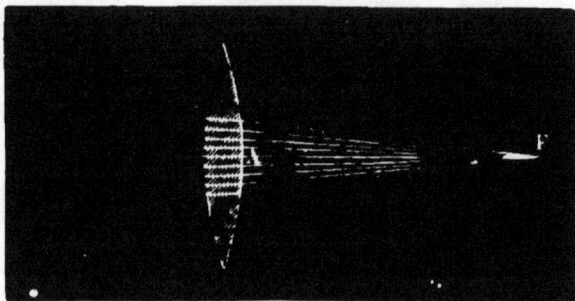

The point F (Fig. 52), where the parallel rays are collected, is called the principal focus of the lens.

What effect is produced on diverging rays ?—We may suppose the rays to *go from* the focus to the lens: these rays (F A, Fig. 52) are diverging, and, as the figure represents them, they will be parallel after going through the lens.

But diverging rays are not always made parallel; indeed, they will not be unless they start from the focus. If they start from a point between the focus and the lens they

Fig. 53.

will diverge after going through, but the divergence will
be less than before. On the other hand, if the rays start
from a point farther than the focus from the lens, they
will be converging after refraction. This case is beautifully shown in Fig. 53.

Does the concave lens have the same effect?—
The concave lens has exactly the opposite effect. The
rays after passing through a concave lens are separated
instead of being collected.

Fig. 54.

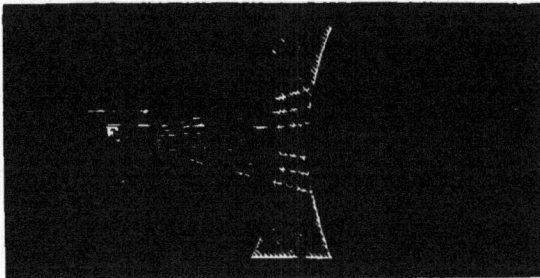

This effect is well shown in Fig. 54, which represents
a double concave lens refracting parallel rays of light.

Fig. 55.

They are supposed to enter the lens on the side F, parallel
to each other, but on coming out on the other side they

are diverging. All the concave lenses have the effect to separate rays by refraction. ·

Describe the image formed by a convex lens.—Most perfect and very beautiful images are formed by the use of convex lenses. If one of these instruments is held at a little distance from any object, a flower, for example, it will form an image which may be caught upon a screen placed in the right spot. This image will be on the other side of the lens from the object, and inverted (Fig. 55).

Explain the production of the image.—Fig. 56 and Fig. 57 will help us to understand how this image is

Fig. 56.

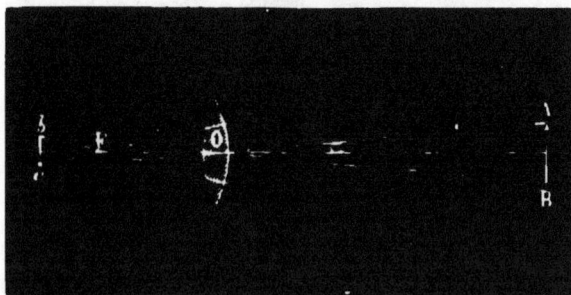

formed. They show a lens with a small arrow, *a b*, near to it. Two rays of light are seen going from *a* through the lens, and after refraction meeting again at A. This point, A, is the image of the point, *a*, from which the rays started. Two other rays are seen going from *b* through the lens and being refracted to the point B. This point B is the image of the other end of the arrow. Every point between *a* and *b* in the arrow will send off rays of light which, after going through the lens, will be brought together again at corresponding points between A and B, and all together they make up the whole image A B.

When will the image be larger than the object ?

—If the image is farther than the object from the lens (see Fig. 56), it will be larger than the object.

When will it be smaller?—But if the image is nearer to the lens than the object is (see Fig. 57), it will be smaller.

Fig. 57.

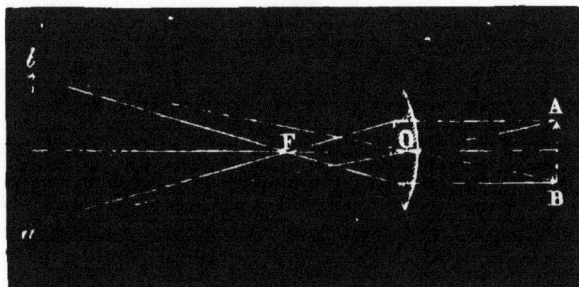

Whichever is farthest from the lens will be the largest.

Will the image ever be on the same side of the lens as the object?—In the cases thus far examined we suppose the object to be outside or beyond the focus of the lens. If the object is put between the lens and its focus, the image will be seen on the same side as the object. It will be erect, and very much larger than the object. In Fig. 58 this case is shown. A small insect is between the focus F, and the lens, and a person looking

Fig. 58.

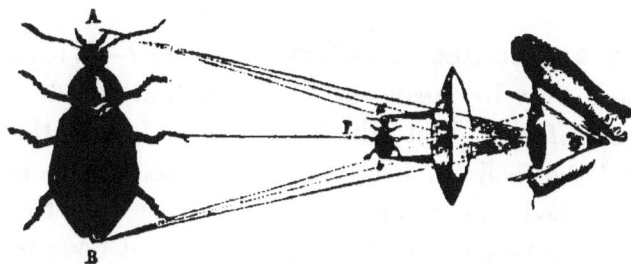

through the lens, ins'ead of seeing the little creature *a b*, will behold its magnified image, A B.

What is the effect of concave lenses?—Concave lenses have just the opposite effect; they form an image always smaller than the object. In Fig. 59 we can see

Fig. 59.

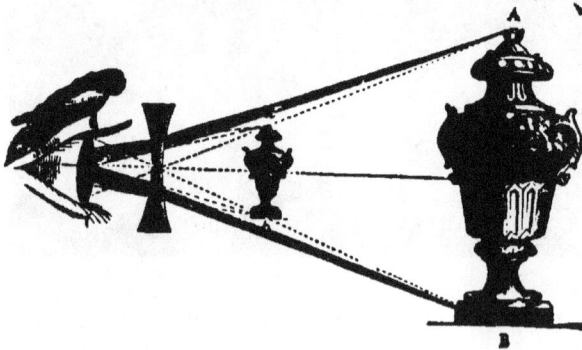

how this is done. The light from the vase A B, after going through the concave lens, seems, to the eye, to have come from the smaller image *a b*.

Is all light of the same color?—The light which the sun sheds upon all things so freely, is said to be *white* light, but yet all light is not white. The light of some stars, for example, is as *red* as a flame of fire, while others shed upon us a delicate light as green as that of an emerald.

Why are bodies of different colors?—We can see an object only by means of the light that is reflected by it. Now, if the light which it reflects is red, then the color of the body is itself red. If a body reflects blue light, the body has a blue color; in every case the color of a body is the color of the light which that body reflects.

The meadows are green because the vegetation throws green light to our eyes.

What curious experiment will illustrate this?— "Fill a spirit-lamp with alcohol in which a large quantity of salt has been dissolved; on being lit it will be found to burn with a livid yellow flame." Let a room be lighted entirely by one or two of such lamps. "It should, if possible, be hung with pictures in water and oil colors, and the persons present ought to wear nothing but the brightest colors, and the table be ornamented with the gayest of flowers." Let the lamps be brought into this darkened room, and an astonishing appearance will be presented. "The furniture and every other object which the room contains will reflect but a single color. The brightest purple, the purest lilac, the liveliest green will be converted into a monotonous yellow. The same change will take place in the countenances of those present: every one will laugh at the appearance of his neighbor's face without thinking that he is just as great a subject of laughter to them."

Nothing can, better than this experiment, show that bodies will seem to be of the color which they can reflect. When they receive only yellow rays, they can themselves be of no other color. And if any of them are not able to reflect yellow light, these will appear black.

Then why, in the sunlight, are not all bodies white?—All bodies in the sunlight are receiving only white light, and if white light was like that of any other color they would all be white. The white light must *contain all other colors* which bodies reflect. These bodies receive all these colors alike, and then each one makes choice of the color which it will reflect. A rose gets white light from the sun, and then from among all the colors it contains, it reflects the red only. A violet reflects blue instead of red or any other, while the leaves of a tree reflect only the green rays of the white light which the sun sheds upon them.

By what instrument can sunlight be separated into its colors?—The instrument used in the arts to decompose light is called a *prism*. It is generally nothing

Fig. 60.

more than a triangular piece of glass, but it may be made of many other substances. Fig. 60 represents the prism, and Fig. 61 shows how this instrument is often mounted upon a stand to be convenient for use.

Describe the experiment with the prism.—Let a prism be held in a beam of sunlight as it enters a darkened room; the rays which come through the prism will strike the wall or ceiling of the room, or upon a screen, and form there a patch of beautifully colored light (Fig. 62). All the colors of the rainbow will be seen; and what is still more beautiful, if dust be sprinkled into the air of the room, these colors will be seen reaching all the

way from the prism to the wall. Rays of purest blue, of
most delicate violet, of the brightest yellow, with others

Fig. 61.

of different colors, will be seen spread out like a fan from
the prism through the dusty air

This arrangement of colors formed from the sunlight
which passes through a prism is called the *solar spectrum*.

What are the colors in the solar spectrum?—
There are *seven* colors in the solar spectrum. They are
arranged in the following order: red, orange, yellow,
green, blue, indigo, and violet.

These are the colors of which sunlight is composed, and
the colors of all bodies in the world are produced by the
mixture of two or more of these in different proportions.

Will the seven colors produce white light?—If

the colors formed by a prism are made to pass through
a double convex lens (Fig. 63) they will be brought
together again and the spot of light upon the wall will be
white. The prism decomposes the white light and brings

Fig. 62.

out the colors: the convex lens combines the colors and
makes white light again. Here, then, is a double proof

Fig. 63.

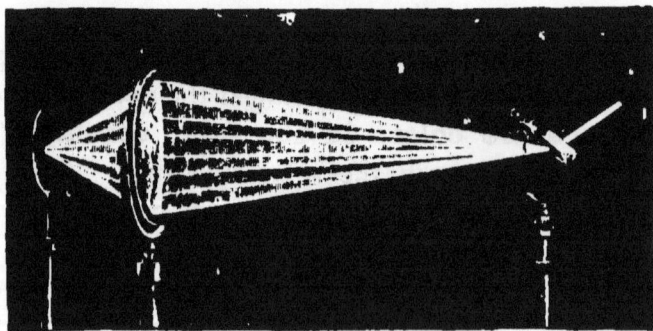

that white light is made up of the seven colors of the
spectrum.

How is the rainbow formed?—In a shower of rain each drop of water is able to decompose the sunlight and give the different colors of the spectrum. This it will do if the sun is shining brightly at the time the drop is falling, and you will remember that all the rainbows you ever saw were seen while the sun was shining. When the sun is behind you, and a shower is falling in front of you, the rays which pass through each drop are decomposed and the colors come out in such a direction that some of them enter your eye. Some drops send the red color to the eye : others in a different place send orange and others still send yellow; another set gives blue, another indigo, and finally another violet. And these seven colors are so arranged as to form the beautiful " bow of promise."

OPTICAL INSTRUMENTS.

What does Fig. 58 represent?—By turning back to Fig. 58, we see that a convex lens when held between the eye and a little insect will help us to see a very large image instead of the little creature itself. Try it yourself by taking grandmother's spectacles, if you have no other lens, and hold one of the glasses just at the right place, which you can find by moving it back and forth between your eye and the page of the book. The letters will look much larger than they really are.

A double convex lens used in this way is called a *simple microscope.*

This little instrument, by making every little thing look larger than it is, becomes a very pleasant, and at the same time a very useful, instrument to every body. Most people use it for viewing fine engravings and in looking at photographs. The watch-maker uses it to examine the minute parts of his work, and the jeweler uses it also for the same purpose.

What is the compound microscope ?—The compound microscope is an instrument by which to see the images of objects which are so very small that the eye alone may not see them at all.

Describe it.—It contains more than one lens; in its simplest form it has two. We can understand it best by studying Fig. 64. Let us begin at the bottom, and notice first a concave mirror. We see the rays of sunlight which fall on this mirror are thrown upward and brought together at *a*. Now the little object to be magnified is placed at this point and the bright light which goes up from it must pass through the lens *b*, which is very near to it. This lens would magnify the object, but not enough, and so the light after going through it is made to go through another larger lens B, and then into the eye of the person. The little thing at the point *a* is made to look large enough to fill all the space between C and D.

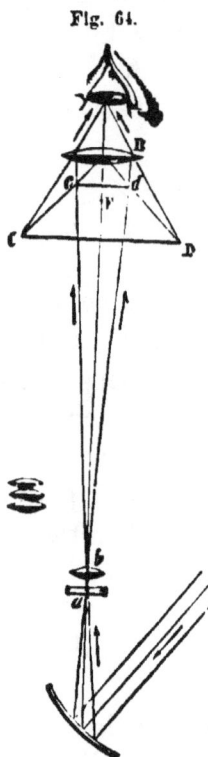

Fig. 64.

What are the lenses called ?—The lens *b* is called the *object-glass*, and the other, near the eye, is called the *eye-piece*. The eye-piece is often made of two lenses and the object-glass sometimes of as many as eight.

How much will this instrument magnify?—By this instrument we are able to make the diameter of the image 2,000 times greater than the real diameter of the object, and in that case the *surface* of the image would be 4,000,000 times as large as that of the object examined! "Under such a power a hair would appear about six inches thick, a fine needle would look like a street-post, and a grain of sand like a mass of rock." Such power is only necessary in examining the very smallest objects. All common preparations are best examined with a power which makes the diameter appear to be only 500 or 600 times larger than it really is.

What has the microscope revealed?—This instrument has made known a world of little things around us which no human eye could ever see without its help. Little animals, and little plants, so very small that thousands of them together would not be as large as the smallest particle of dust you ever saw, are almost everywhere in the soil and water and other substances around us.

What is a telescope?—The telescope is an instrument by which we are able to examine objects which are so far away that the eye alone can not see them distinctly. It contains lenses or mirrors by which the images of distant objects are made near to the eye.

Describe one kind.—We can describe one kind of

Fig. 61.

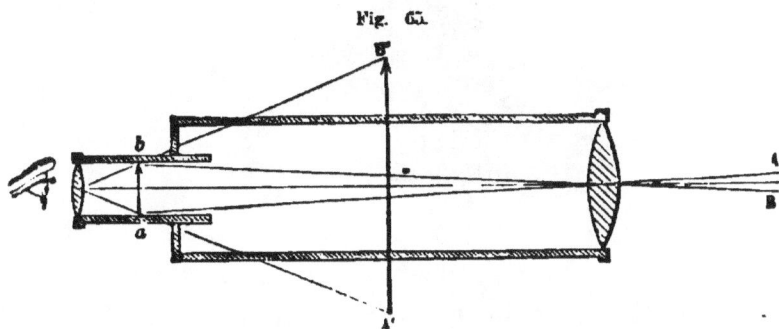

telescope best by means of the foregoing diagram, Fig 65. A large convex lens is in one end of a tube and a smaller one is at the other end. This small one is the *eye-glass*, and can be moved back and forth so as to be fixed at just the right distance from the other. The light from a distant body coming through the large lens forms an image at *a b*, and then a person looking through the eye-glass sees this image magnified at A' B'.

Fig. 66.

The tube containing these glasses is mounted in some way to allow it to be pointed toward any object in the heavens. The picture, Fig. 66, shows a small one. One of the largest of this kind of telescope in the world is at Harvard College. Its object-glass is about eighteen inches in diameter.

What has the telescope revealed?—The telescope has made known a great many things about the sun and moon and stars. It has shown that the moon is covered with mountains and valleys; and that the sun has immense black spots on its surface that looks to us so bright. It shows that there are hosts of stars in the sky, which could never have been seen without its help, some of them being so far away that light, travelling fast enough to go around the world about seven times a second, would need many hundreds of years to come from them to us.

6*

HEAT.

What is the chief source of heat?—From the sun more heat is received than from all other sources together. It is more than 90,000,000 of miles from the earth, and yet there comes out through that vast distance a constant flood of heat which, if withdrawn for a single year, would leave the whole earth in a degree of cold which even the Arctic regions never had.

What is a source of artificial heat?—Combustion is the chief source of artificial heat. Wood, coal, or other fuel burning in our stoves or furnaces warms our dwellings, cooks our food, and makes the steam by which our machinery is driven. Next to the sun, combustion is certainly the most important source of heat.

How is the heat in combustion produced?—If you shut the draught of an "air-tight" stove the fire will go out; or, if you put a lighted candle under the receiver of an air-pump, it will die away when the air is exhausted. We learn from such experiments that *no fuel can burn without air.* Unless air can pass over the hot fuel in the stove there can be no fire.

Now the air is made up of two parts which the chemist calls oxygen and nitrogen, and it is the *oxygen* of the air passing over the fuel which causes the combustion. The oxygen unites itself to the carbon and other materials of which the fuel consists, and to this action the heat of the fire is due.

What is another source of heat ?—Mechanical action, such as rubbing or pounding, will produce heat. Let the fingers be pressed down upon the table, and then smartly rubbed back and forth: the heat caused by this friction will be quickly felt. Or if a small cord or a thread is swiftly drawn through the hand which holds it tightly, the hand will be cruelly burned. If two pieces of wood are rubbed upon each other briskly enough they may be set on fire; in this way savage people are said to have kindled their fires: more civilized people now do it more easily by simply rubbing the end of a match.

Blows also produce heat, as any one may easily prove by pounding a bullet with a hammer, for he can soon make it too hot to be comfortably held in the hand.

Does heat pass from one body to another ?—From every heated body rays of heat are continually going away. This is almost too familiar to need illustration, for the stove gives its warmth to all other objects in the room, and a red-hot cannon-ball will part with its heat so rapidly as to very soon get dark and finally cold.

But there is this curious fact to add to what has just been said : no body is at any time so cold that it is not giving off heat to every other around it. Heat is constantly passing away from every body, no matter how cold it may already be, and what is given off by one is being received by others in its neighborhood, so that it is true that even a block of ice is giving heat to a red-hot stove, if placed in its vicinity.

Then why do hot bodies grow colder ?—Now if the ice and the stove in this illustration should each give off just as much heat as it gets from the other back again, the ice would not melt nor the stove grow cold. But the hot stove is giving off much more than it gets, and on this account it becomes gradually colder if the fire is not kept up, while, at the same time, the ice gets much more than it gives, and is of course melted by it.

A body gets warmer only when it is getting heat from others faster than it is giving heat to them: it gets colder only when it gives heat faster than it gets it.

How does heat get from one body to another ?— Heat travels outward from a hot body in waves something like the motion of water-waves when a pebble is thrown into a pond or lake. As the pebble puts the water in motion, so the hot body gives motion to the substance which fills the space around it; and as the waves of water spread outward in all directions from the pebble, so the waves of heat spread in all directions from their source. These waves of heat warm every body against which they strike.

With what velocity do these waves travel?— And they go from one body to another so very swiftly that one can not measure the small instant of time they take to pass through any common distance. They start from a hot stove and at the same instant they seem to strike the face of a person in the most distant corner of the room. Indeed, their velocity is so great that they would be able to go quite around the world as many as seven times in a single second! The velocity of heat is like that of light: together they come to us from the sun, a distance of more than 90,000,000 miles, in about 8 minutes. This would be at the rate of about 190,000 miles a second.

What name is given to heat sent off by bodies in

this way?—The heat which travels in this way is called *radiant heat*. Its peculiarities are, when briefly stated, *first*, it goes in straight lines; *second*, it goes in all possible directions from its source; and *third*, it moves with very great velocity.

This mode of transferring heat from place to place is called *radiation*.

Is there another mode?—Heat does not always travel in this way. If you take one of grandmother's knitting needles and hold one end of it in a lamp-flame you will feel the other very soon getting warm. The heat enters the metal at one end and travels, step by step, from one particle to another until at length it reaches the fingers. In this way it is carried from one part of a body to another, or it may be from one body to another, if they touch each other. This mode of transferring heat is called *conduction*.

Do all solids conduct heat alike?—If we take two wires of equal size and length, one being of copper and the other of iron, and place one end of each in a flame, we shall find that the heat travels through the copper to the other end quicker than through the iron. Copper conducts heat better than iron does. A rod of glass may be melted within an inch of the fingers that hold it without burning them, and a splinter of wood may be held in the same way while it burns to ashes.

We thus learn that each solid has a rate of its own at which it may conduct heat. Liquids scarcely conduct it at all, and gases in a degree still less.

Bodies that conduct heat freely are called good conductors, but those that do not are called poor conductors or non-conductors.

Are liquids and gases conductors of heat?—Water is so very poor a conductor of heat that if you put

ice at the bottom of a glass vessel and then apply heat to
the water above it, Fig. 67, you may make the water boil

Fig. 67.

Fig. 68.

without melting the ice; the heat will not travel down-ward through the water to the ice. Other liquids, except mercury, are like water in being very poor conductors of heat.

Gases are still poorer conductors than liquids.

What is one effect caused by heat?—Let us learn by experiment what effect heat pro-duces:

1st. In solids. A ball of iron or of brass is taken just large enough to pass easily through a ring of the same material. The ball is then heated by a lamp, after which it will be too large to go through the ring. It will rest upon the ring (Fig. 68) until it gets cold again, when it once more passes easily as at first. We see that heat makes this ball larger. And it has the same effect upon other solids.

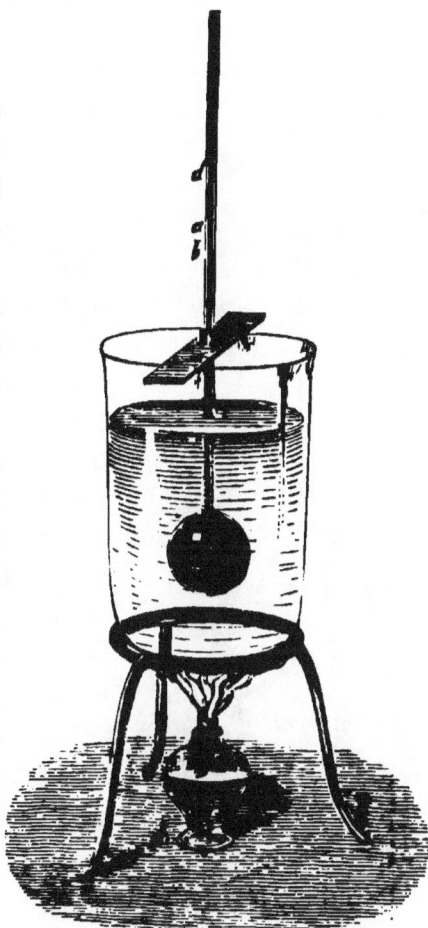

Fig. 69.

2d. Liquids. A glass bulb with a long open stem is used. The bulb is filled with water and the stem partly filled, after which, if the bulb is plunged into hot water (Fig. 69), the water in the stem will be seen slowly rising, until perhaps it will run over the top. The water grows larger as it gets warmer. We see that heat expands this liquid: it does the same thing for others.

3d. Gases. Fig. 70 shows an experiment with air.

Fig. 70.

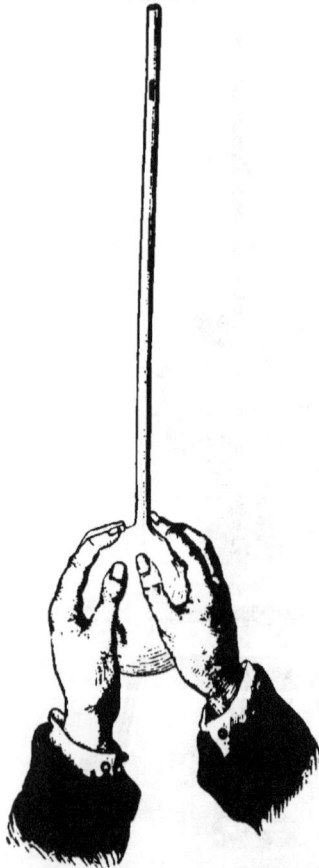

The glass bulb with its long open stem is used for this also. The little black spot near the end of the tube represents a little drop of ink which has been put into the tube and which will be held there by the walls of glass. Now when the warm hands take hold of the bulb the drop will run up still higher in the tube. The air below it pushes the ink up because it wants more room. The heat of the hand makes the air larger than it was. Heat also expands all other gases.

We learn from these experiments that the general effect of heat is to expand all bodies to which it is applied.

What facts illustrate the expansion of solids ?—An iron gate which opens and shuts easily in cold weather, will stick, in a warm day, owing to the heat which expands it. Pipes of cast-iron for conveying hot water are longer when full than when empty. It is said that an ignorant man once tried to warm a large manufactory by steam. He laid one large iron pipe from the boiler to the farther end of the building, and then passed branches from this through holes into the several rooms. The very first time he filled the pipes with steam, the expansion of the main pipe tore it away from all its branches !

The rails of a railroad-track are longer in summer than in winter.

What facts illustrate the expansion of liquids?— A kettle nearly full of cold water will be quite full when the water is heated: the water will run over long before it boils.

Twenty gallons of alcohol in midwinter will become about twenty-one gallons in midsummer. Hence cunning dealers try to make purchases in winter and sales in summer, that the heat of summer may add to their profits.

Does heat always expand water?—At all temperatures above 39° water will be expanded by applying *heat*, but at temperatures below 39° water will be *contracted* by applying heat. At 39° a given weight of water is as small as it can be; heat it or cool it as you will, and it will be expanded.

Are all liquids like water in this respect?—To show how different are the effects of a change of temperature in water and other liquids, the following experiment is made. Three glass globes with long necks are placed in a large dish nearly filled with ice-cold water (Fig. 71).

Suppose the water cooled to 32°?—At 32° the *water freezes.* The expansion at this moment is greater than at any moment before, so that the *ice* is *larger* than the *water* from which it is made.

On this account pitchers and water-pipes are often broken by the water freezing in them.

Ice being larger must also be *lighter* than the water from which it is made. Were it not for this fact our ponds and rivers would never be covered with a blanket

of ice as now they are in the winter. The ice, instead,
would sink to the bottom as fast as formed. There could
be no skating then, you notice; but that would not be the

Fig. 71.

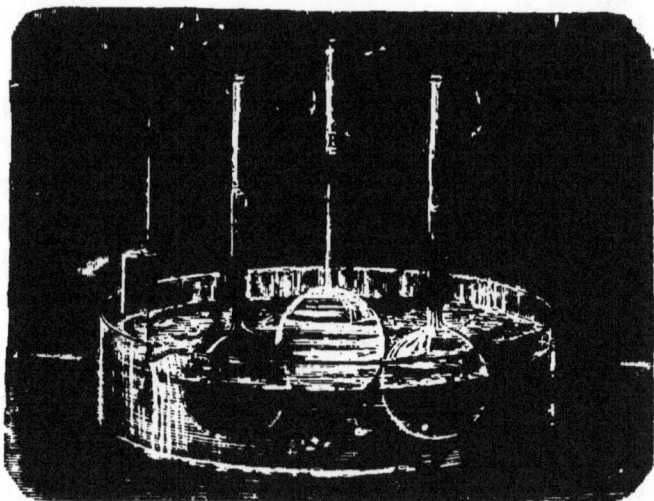

saddest of the story, for there would soon be no human
beings to enjoy that or any other sport. As it now is, the
ice stays on top and keeps the water from freezing to any
great depth; but if it should sink, it would go on forming
until the whole body of water would become ice from
bottom to top, and then the atmosphere would get colder
and colder, until neither plants nor animals could live
at all.

What facts illustrate the expansion of air?—The
snapping of wood in the fire is caused by the expansion
of air. The air in the pores of the wood, suddenly heated,
expands and bursts the wood with a sharp report.

The first balloons that were made were filled with hot
air, and they went up toward and even above the clouds,

because the air they contained was expanded and made lighter than the cold air—so light that it could rise and carry the balloon up with it. Only toy-balloons are now filled with hot air; those by which men are carried to the clouds are filled with common illuminating gas, or sometimes with hydrogen.

Which is most expanded by heat, solids, liquids, or gases?—A little addition of heat expands a gas very much; the same applied to a liquid would cause an increase in size difficult to see, and if it were applied to a solid, would not change its size enough to be noticed at all.

Do all solids and liquids expand equally?—Instead of all solids expanding equally, each one has a certain rate of its own. Brass for example, will expand faster than iron. Each liquid also has a rate of its own.

Do all gases expand equally?—Gases all expand alike by heat. Air, oxygen, and all other gases, heated alike, will expand equally.

What is a second effect of heat?—If iron is heated it will go on expanding long after it has become red-hot, until finally it *melts*. The solid is then changed into a liquid; this is a second effect of heat. It is called *liquefaction*.

Do all solids melt at the same temperature?—A few examples which all have noticed will show that solids melt at very different temperatures. The warmth of the hand will melt ice, but not wax. Sulphur will melt on a hot stove; it needs a temperature of 230°, but iron does not melt until it is heated to about 3,000°. Each substance has a certain temperature at which it melts. This temperature is called the *melting-point*.

What is a third effect of heat ?—If water is heated it will go on expanding until its temperature is 212° : at this temperature it *boils*. The liquid is then changed into a gas; this is a third effect of heat. It is called *vaporization*.

Do all liquids boil at the same temperature ?—Water boils in an open iron vessel at the temperature of 212°, but alcohol will boil at 173°, and ether only needs to be heated to 95°. These illustrations show that each liquid has its own degree of heat at which it boils: this temperature is called the *boiling-point*.

Describe the experiment in which, by cooling the vessel, water is made to boil.—A very curious experiment is represented in Fig. 72. In the first place a

Fig. 72.

glass bulb with long open stem is partly filled with water. This water is then boiled for some time until the steam has driven all the air out of the vessel. While the water is still boiling, the stem is tightly corked and the heat taken away at the same moment. All this is done to get rid of the air and leave nothing but water and steam in the vessel. The bulb is then turned upward as in the picture. After this *pour cold water* upon the bulb, and *the water inside will boil* vigorously. Stop pouring cold water and the boiling will cease, but as often as the cold is applied the boiling will begin. This may be kept up until the vessel is cold enough to be held in the hand without inconvenience.

What does the cold water do?—Now all that the cold water does is to cool the steam that is in the bulb and condense it into water. By this means the *pressure* of the steam is taken off from the water inside.

Describe another experiment in which water is made to boil without fire.—The pressure may be taken from the surface of the water in another way. The water is put into a flask, to the top of which is fastened a long tube. This arrangement is shown in Fig. 73. The

Fig. 73.

water is then heated until it begins to boil. The flask is then taken from the fire and its tube is fastened to the plate of the air-pump. On working the pump, the air and steam are taken from the flask, and the water, which by this time is much below 212°, begins to boil violently.

What do these experiments teach?—We learn from these experiments that by taking pressure away from the surface of water, boiling will go on at a lower temperature.

In the open air water boils at 212°, but the pressure of the atmosphere is 15 lbs. upon each square inch of surface. If it were not for this pressure water would boil at a temperature much lower than 212°, indeed at a temperature not much above that of a hot summer day.

Water boils at a low temperature on top of high mountains. In fact, at places very high above the level of the sea, boiling water is not hot enough to cook meat, or even to boil eggs, because the pressure of the atmosphere is so much less than at the sea-level.

Suppose the pressure is increased?—On the other hand, if water is heated under a greater pressure than that of the atmosphere, the boiling-point will be higher than 212°. In a word, the boiling-point is *raised* by increasing the pressure and *lowered* by lessening it.

Does steam exert pressure?—Steam often lifts the lid of a kettle in order to make its escape, and when confined in a boiler, it sometimes bursts the stoutest bands of iron, killing people and destroying buildings by the force of the explosion. Such facts show that steam can exert a great pressure when confined.

How can it be used to move machinery?—If there is a piston moving freely inside of a cylinder, and then if steam is let into the cylinder, first at one end and then at the other, its expansive force or pressure will knock the piston back and forth from one end to the other with great rapidity and power. The piston may move a crank which turns a wheel, and then by bands or cogs this wheel may turn other wheels. In this way steam is made to move machinery. This is the principle of the *steam-engine*, by which ships are driven over the sea and railroad trains across the continent, and by which so much of all the machinery in the world is moved.

Can water be heated above 212°?—If water is slowly heated its temperature will rise until the liquid boils at 212°: after that the water grows no hotter. The fire may be quickened and the boiling will be more violent, but the water will not become any hotter. This is always true when the water is heated in open vessels such as are generally used.

What becomes of the heat added to the boiling water?—Now the fire gives heat to the boiling water all the time, but, as we see, does not make it any hotter. All the heat that goes into the water is then used *in changing the water into steam.*

Can we get this heat back again?—All this heat which has been used to change the water into steam, will be given up when the steam changes back into water. This is the reason that a plate grows hot so very quickly when held in the steam that issues from the spout of the tea-kettle.

Is this principle ever applied?—Buildings are sometimes warmed by steam. From a large steam-boiler cast-iron pipes are laid to the many rooms to be warmed, and the steam is forced through their entire length. The steam is condensed in going through the cold pipes, and gives up to them the heat which it took from the fire. They very soon become very warm, and warm the air which is in contact with them.

Do we know the temperature of bodies by feeling them?—Let us take three vessels of water, one almost as cold as ice, another just warmer than the hand, and a

third as hot as the hand can bear.   Let one hand be held
in the first vessel of cold water and the other in the vessel
of hot water for a while, and then let both be plunged
into the vessel of warm water.   It will be found that to
one hand the water is cold, to the other it is hot, at the
same time.   Of course, by the feeling we could not tell
whether it is really hot or cold.

Give another example.—An oil-cloth and a carpet,
where they lie together upon the floor, are of the same
temperature, but the oil-cloth will feel cold and the carpet
warm to the hand at the same time.

The reason of this is that the oil-cloth is a better conductor of heat than the carpet, and takes the heat of the
hand away faster, so that the hand grows cold quicker
when upon it.

**By what instrument can we find the tempera-
ture of bodies ?**—The instruments by which to measure
temperature are called *thermometers*.   The common thermometer contains mercury, which expands when heated,
and contracts when cooled, and by these changes of
volume shows the temperature.

Describe the common thermometer.—The thermometer is very common, and a single look at it would
be better than any description of it can be.   However, it
may be described as a glass tube, with a bulb at one end,
while the other end is shut air-tight, containing mercury
which fills the bulb and part of the stem, and having a
scale behind the stem to show the height of the fluid.
Fig. 74 shows two forms of this instrument.

How is it used ?—By putting the bulb into water or
any other substance the height of the mercury in the stem
will show how hot it is.   Put the bulb in water, for instance, and if the mercury rises in the stem up to the

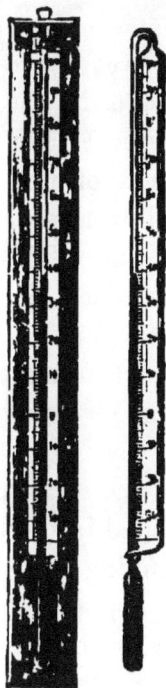
Fig. 74.

place marked 90 on the scale, then the temperature of the water is 90°.

How is Fahrenheit's thermometer graduated?—The place where the mercury stands when the bulb is immersed in boiling water is marked 212° on the scale; where the mercury stands when the bulb is immersed in freezing water is marked 32°: the space between these is divided into 180 equal parts, called degrees, and divisions of the same size are marked off on the scale both above and below these points.

How is the centigrade thermometer graduated?—In the centigrade thermometer, the place where the mercury stands when the bulb is placed in boiling water is marked 100°; where it stands when the bulb is in freezing water is called 0°, and the distance between is divided into 100 equal parts or degrees.

7

MAGNETISM.

What is a loadstone ?—Several hundred years ago pieces of a certain kind of iron ore were found in the earth which had the power to attract bits of iron. They would lift needles or small nails or other bits of iron which they touched, and hold them suspended in the air as if they were cemented to the stone with glue. The ore of iron which has this wonderful power is called the *loadstone*. It is found sometimes in this country, but not in such abundance as in Sweden and Norway, and in some parts of Asia. A good specimen may be bought for a few cents, and it is an interesting and instructive toy. It is often called the *natural magnet*.

What is a magnet ?—If a loadstone is rolled in iron filings it will attract them and hold them clinging to its surface, but when rolled in filings of brass or copper not one of these will it pick up. It has a curious preference for iron. Any body that will attract iron in preference to other metals is called a *magnet*.

What are artificial magnets ?—A bar of steel may be made a magnet by simply rubbing it upon the loadstone. In this way the blade of a penknife may be given the power to pick up bits of iron, such as small needles, tacks, or iron filings. One blade can get this power also from another which has been already made magnetic; and what is a little singular, perhaps, is that the one that gives this power to another is none the weaker for it; it is even stronger than before. All such pieces of steel are magnets.

Iron also may be made magnetic, but it will not stay so unless it be first hardened more than usual.

In what two shapes are magnets made?—Artificial magnets are made in two forms. They are generally either a straight bar of steel or else a bar bent into the form of a horse-shoe. The first is called the *bar magnet*, and the second is called the *horse-shoe* magnet.

What is an armature?—A horse-shoe magnet generally has with it a bar of iron to reach across from one end of the magnet to the other. Such a bar is called the *armature*.

In what part of a magnet is the attraction strongest?—By rolling a bar magnet in a bed of iron filings and then lifting it, the filings may be seen clinging to the ends of the bar in curious tufts (Fig. 75), while along the middle few or none will be found.

Fig. 75.

This experiment shows the power of the magnet to be much greater at the ends than elsewhere. The ends of the magnet, or the points at which the force is strongest, are called the *poles*.

. Fig. 76 represents a horse-shoe magnet with an armature across the poles holding up a heavy weight.

What is the magnetic needle?—A slender bar magnet balanced upon a pivot (Fig. 77) is called a *magnetic needle*.

Left to itself, such a needle will always be found pointing toward the north and south. It will not rest in any other position. If you push it out of this direction it will swing back again the moment you let go of it, and after vibrating from one side to the other for a time, it will at last come to rest again with *the same end* to the north as before.

Fig. 76.

The end that points toward the north is called the *north pole:* the other end is called the *south pole.*

What use is made of the magnetic needle? — What is called the mariner's compass is a magnetic needle placed over a dial on which are marked north, south, east, west, and many other directions, or as they are called, " points of the compass." This little instrument is placed where it will be every moment in view of the man who guides the ship, and tells him every moment in what direction the ship is going.

No matter how dark the night or how rough the sea may be, the faithful needle, pointing always so nearly north and south, guides the storm-tossed seaman safely to his port.

What is a dipping needle?—If a magnetic needle is hung in a way to let its poles move up and down it will not rest in a horizontal position. The picture (Fig. 78) shows what direction it will take: the north pole will be lower than the other. A needle fixed in this way is called a *dipping needle.*

Is the dip of the needle everywhere alike?—The

dip of the needle is not the same in all places on the earth. In the most northern regions the needle is most oblique, that is to say, the dip is greatest. Just at the north pole the needle would point its north pole downward to the ground. As the needle is carried farther to the south the north pole rises until when at the equator the needle would be horizontal, or have no dip at all, and then when carried farther into the southern hemisphere the south pole would dip instead of the north pole.

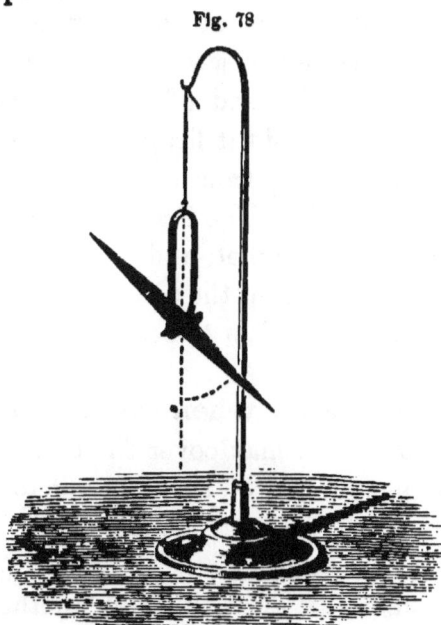

Fig. 77.

Fig. 78

How will one magnet act upon another?

Let one magnet be brought near to another; suppose, for instance, that you hold one in the hand and point its *north* pole toward the *south* pole of the magnetic needle. They will quickly come together: if in reach of each other they can not be kept apart. These unlike poles *attract* each other.

Next point the *north* pole toward the *north* pole of the needle, and it will swing quickly away, so that it will be almost impossible to make the two magnets touch each other. These poles of the same name *repel* each other.

State the law of attraction and repulsion?—It will always be the case as in the experiments just described, that *poles of unlike names attract each other, while poles of the same name repel each other.*

Describe the experiment to illustrate induction. —Hold a strong magnet in a vertical position and touch the lower pole with the end of a much smaller bar of iron: the magnet will hold it firmly in the air. Another smaller bar may be hung from the lower end of the first, and another yet from it. The first bar of iron receives its magnetism from the magnet, and then the second from the first and the third from the second. This power of a magnet to impart magnetism to other bars of iron or steel is called *induction.*

Will induction occur when the magnet does not touch the iron?—We may cover the end of the magnet with paper so that the bar of iron can not touch the pole, and yet find that it becomes a magnet by induction as before.

Or we may show this same thing by another and more curious experiment. Let a horse-shoe magnet be placed poles upward, and lay across its ends a piece of stiff card-board or a piece of glass. Sprinkle iron filings upon the cardboard and at the same time gently tap it with the finger. The filings will then be seen to collect in clusters around the poles of the magnet and to arrange themselves in strange curves from pole to pole.

Now in this experiment each little filing becomes a magnet by induction through the card or glass, and then each pole of one attracts the opposite pole of its neighbor, so that they cling to each other in curves and clusters

Describe the experiment with the glass rod.—
Fig. 79 shows the results of an easy and amusing experiment. A glass rod, or perhaps a stick of sealing-wax, must be rubbed briskly with a flannel cloth for a few

Fig. 79.

moments, and then held near to pieces of some light substance, such as bits of cotton or balls of pith taken from the elder-bush or corn-stalk. These light bodies will quickly jump upward against the rod, and then, as if disappointed with their visit, as quickly jump away again.

What does this experiment show?—We see by this experiment that rubbing glass with flannel gives to the glass a power which it did not have before—the power to attract and to repel light substances.

What is this power called?—This new power aroused in the glass is called *electricity*. In this case the electricity is produced by *friction*.

Does friction always produce electricity?—Whenever substances are rubbed together electricity is evolved. And yet if an iron rod is used in place of the glass in the experiment (Fig. 79), the pith balls will not stir from the table, because the electricity flies along the surface of the iron and away through the hand as fast as it is produced.

What are conductors and non-conductors?—All bodies which will allow electricity to pass over their surfaces freely are called *conductors* of electricity. Iron is a good conductor, and so are other metals and many common substances besides.

Bodies which, like glass, will not allow electricity to pass freely over them are called *non-conductors*. Besides glass many other common substances are non-conductors. Air is one of the most perfect of them all. And among others it is well to mention India-rubber, sealing-wax, and silk.

What is an electroscope?—An instrument to detect the presence of electricity in any body is called an *electroscope*. Fig. 80 will give a good idea of one of these instruments. It is only a little ball of pith hung by a silk cord from the end of a standard.

The glass rod, after being rubbed with the flannel cloth, will show its electricity by attracting the pith-ball. On coming in contact with the glass the pith itself becomes electrified, and then jumps away from the glass.

7*

What is an electric machine ?—The glass rod and sealing-wax will give electricity enough only to show itself distinctly. When it is to be obtained in greater

Fig. 80.

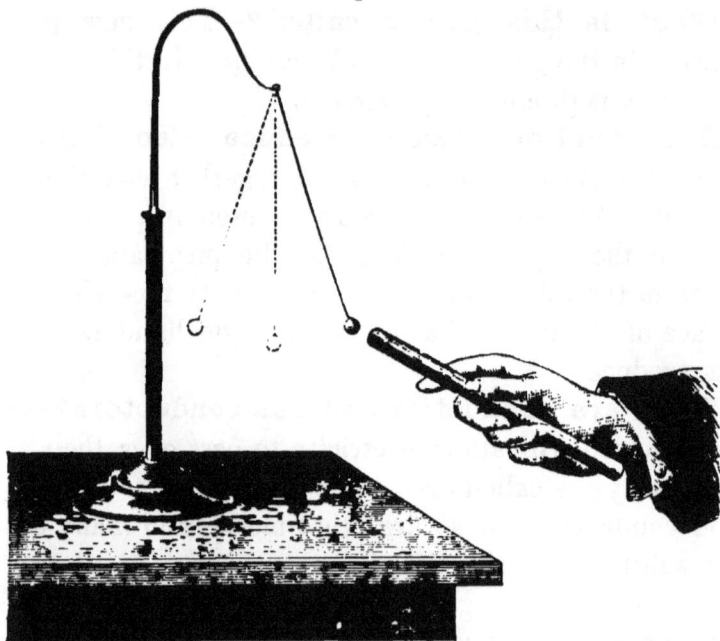

force other apparatus must be used. *Any apparatus by which electricity of considerable force is obtained* may be called an electrical machine.

The most common form of the electrical machine consists of a large circular glass plate, with its axle resting upon pillars. This plate is turned with a crank, and in turning it rubs between two rubbers. This friction gives the electricity. Then there is a brass ball or cylinder resting upon a glass pillar which takes the electricity from the glass plate. This ball or cylinder is called the *prime conductor*, and the electricity for experiments is taken from it.

In what two ways does electricity act?—The experiment with the electroscope described a little while since, shows that electricity acts both by *attraction* and *repulsion*. Look back, and read that experiment again.

Will glass and sealing-wax act alike?—The electroscope will help us to show that the electricity from glass and that from sealing-wax do not act alike.

Let the glass rod be rubbed and once brought in contact with the pith-ball (Fig. 80). The ball will after this be *repelled* by the glass. Next rub a stick of sealing-wax, and then hold it near to the pith: the little ball will quickly fly toward it, being *attracted* by the sealing-wax. Do not let it touch the sealing-wax, and you will find that every time the glass comes near it the ball will be *repelled*, and every time the wax approaches it the ball will be *attracted*. The glass and sealing-wax act in exactly opposite ways.

How are these two actions named?—The electricity of the glass has been called *positive* electricity, and that from the sealing-wax has been called *negative* electricity.

Now, whenever other non-conductors are rubbed, some of them will give positive electricity and others negative electricity. But when we speak of positive electricity we mean simply that it is like the electricity from glass, and the term negative electricity means only that the electricity is like that obtained from sealing-wax.

What is the law of attraction and repulsion?—The action of these two forces is always in obedience to the following law:

Bodies having the same kind of electricity repel each other, but having opposite kinds they attract each other.

Show that electricity is only on the outside surface of a body.—Fig. 81 shows a curious experiment which teaches us where the electricity of a body is to be

Fig. 81.

found. A sack made of muslin and in the shape of a cone is fastened to a metallic ring upon a standard. The sack is to be held out by a long silk cord. When the ring is brought in contact with any body already charged with electricity, the force will spread into the ring and from it into the sack. On examining the sack its *outside* surface will show the presence of electricity, but its *inside* surface will not. Now by taking hold of the other end of the cord the sack may be turned inside out; and, on examining again, the electricity is found to be on what is now the outside, while not a trace of it can be found upon the inside. No matter how often nor how quickly the sack is turned inside-out, the electricity will always be found on the *outside*.

Can a conductor be charged with electricity ?— Since electricity will pass freely over the surface of any conductor, it would at first seem to be impossible to make it remain, or, in other words, to charge the conductor. But let the conductor be placed upon a glass support, and the electricity will have no means of escape, so that it will be compelled to stay.

A body which does not touch any other conducting surface is said to be *insulated.* The electricity can not stay on the surface of any conductor unless it be insulated.

Can a pointed conductor be charged?—A conductor with a pointed wire reaching out from its surface will not retain electricity even when insulated. The force passes off from the point into the air, and seems to be lost.

A candle-flame held in front of such a point will be blown as if struck by a breeze of air, and indeed it is, for the air electrified by the point is repelled and moves away : it is this current of air that wafts the flame.

Suppose a pointed conductor brought near to an electrified body.—If we put the pointed end of a wire near to any body which is electrified it will draw the electricity away without touching it. To point the finger at the prime conductor of an electrical machine will be almost enough to keep the conductor from being charged : and an open penknife held in the hand and pointed at the conductor will be found quite enough to draw away the electricity as fast as it is evolved.

For what purpose are pointed conductors used? —Lightning-rods are *pointed conductors,* which are used to protect buildings from being struck by lightning.

Lightning is nothing more than the *light* caused by electricity in the air or clouds, and thunder is only the *noise* that is made by the electricity when it passes from one cloud to another or to the earth.

When a cloud full of electricity floats along over a house the electricity sometimes leaps into the building and tears it to pieces, or perhaps sets it on fire; but if the house has a good lightning-rod reaching above the roof, the point of the rod will take the electricity out of the cloud silently and gradually, and in this way the disaster may be prevented.

Who first took lightning from the clouds?—Dr. Franklin first drew electricity from the clouds in such a way as to be able to examine it, and prove that lightning is nothing but electricity.

How did he do it?—This discovery of the nature of lightning was one of the most important ever made in the science, and yet, Dr. Franklin made it simply by *flying a kite in a thunder-shower* (Fig. 82).

He made his kite of silk instead of paper, and sent it up with a hempen cord ending in a piece of silk cord, by which the kite was held. It is said that he fastened a door-key to the lower end of the hempen cord, and that after his kite had been for some time sailing among the clouds he touched this key with his knuckle and drew a spark of electricity from it. The electricity in the cloud entered the kite, and came down the hempen string to the key, but could not go any farther because the silk cord was a non-conductor. When the doctor presented his hand the electricity in the key leaped into his knuckle.

Can electricity act through non-conductors?—The following experiment will show that electricity can and will act through non-conductors.

We will suppose the ball C (Fig. 83) to be insulated and charged with electricity. Another insulated conductor, AB, is slowly moved toward the ball, and when the

Fig. 62.

end of it is still at some distance, the pith-balls, which have all the time hung vertically, suddenly jump away and remain as shown in the picture.

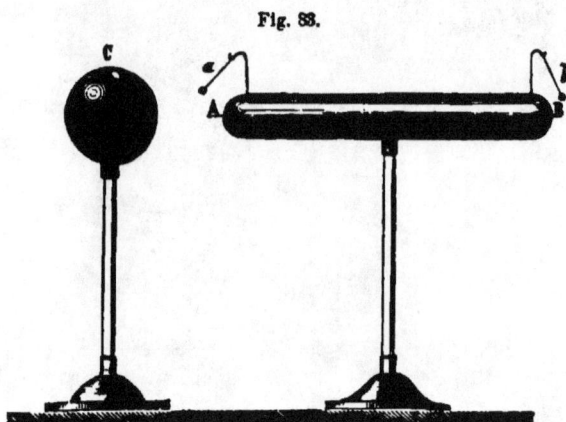

Fig. 83.

The action of the pith-balls shows that the insulated conductor AB is electrified, and we see that the electricity of the ball C must have acted through the air. It would have the same effect through glass or other non-conductors.

What is this action called?—This action of a charged body through non-conductors is called *induction*.

What is its effect?—It will be found that the insulated body AB is not electrified all over its surface alike. *Both kinds of electricity are found upon it.* The ends are most powerfully electrified, and *the two ends are in opposite conditions.* The end B, most distant, has the same kind of electricity as the charged ball C.

Such will always prove to be the case. Induction always causes *both kinds* of electricity to appear on the surface of an insulated body.

How do we describe this condition of an insu-

lated body?—When both kinds of electricity are developed on the surface of a body, it is said to be *polarized*.

Describe the electrical bells.—Fig. 84 shows a chime of bells, which are to be rung by electricity. Notice how they are arranged. The two outside bells are fastened by metal chains to a rod of metal which hangs from the end of the prime conductor of an electrical machine. The middle bell is hung by a silk thread and has a chain passing from it to the floor. Finally, notice two little balls of metal between the bells: these balls are hung by silk threads also. When the machine is in operation, these little balls will fly back and forth and ring the bells loudly.

Fig. 84.

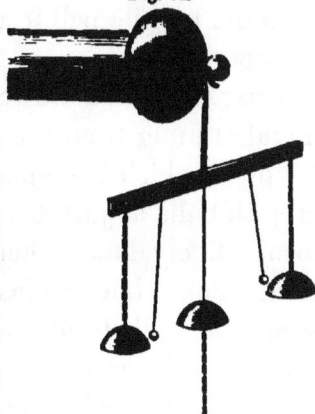

Explain this experiment.—The electricity from the machine passes down the chains into the outside bells, but it can not get into the middle bell nor into the little balls, because their silk cords are not conductors. Now when one outside bell is charged, its electricity will act through the air upon the little ball and *polarize* it, and the electricity on that side of the ball nearest the bell is the other kind from that in the bell itself. Then the two unlike kinds attract each other, and this is what brings the ball to strike the bell.

But when the ball touches the bell it takes electricity from it, and then the two, having the same kind of electricity, repel each other. This is what throws the little ball against the middle bell. But when it touches the middle bell it gives away its electricity and is ready to be polarized over again. It is first *polarized*, then *attracted*, then *repelled* over and over again, perhaps fifty times while we are giving the explanation once.

The chain from the middle bell is to conduct away the electricity brought by the little balls. This is needed to keep the middle bell from becoming charged, and stopping the operation.

Describe the dancing pith-balls.—If a plate of metal is hung from the machine just above another similar plate which lies upon the table, and then if a handful of pith-balls is just between the two, these balls will perform a lively dance whenever the machine is put in operation. Sometimes a glass shade is put over the disks to keep the balls from flying away from between them, as they are otherwise very sure to do.

Each little ball is first polarized by the electricity in the upper plate, and then attracted and afterward repelled.

What do these experiments illustrate?—These experiments illustrate the fact that no light body is ever *attracted* until after it is *polarized* by the charged body toward which it flies.

Describe the charged goblet of water.—A long time ago a gentleman in France was experimenting with electricity to see how it would affect water. A chain from the conductor of his machine hung down into a goblet of the liquid, but it seemed to produce no effect, and he was about to take it away. He seized the goblet in one hand and took hold of the chain with the other. The moment that his fingers touched the chain, he received a shock which convulsed his hands and gave him such a fright that he did not quite get over it in two days.

Explain this experiment.—The water in the goblet was charged with electricity from the machine, and when the hand was placed around the outside, it and the glass were *polarized*, so that the outside and inside of the goblet were in opposite conditions. When the other hand touched the chain the arms and body made a conducting road through which the two electricities could get together, and their action through the person caused the curious and unexpected feeling called the shock.

What should we notice in the arrangement of the goblet?—Now we notice that there were three things—the water *inside*, the hand *outside*, and the glass *between*, and that the water and the hand are good conductors, while the glass is not. To put it in few words, we see that *there were two conductors kept apart by a nonconductor*.

Describe the Leyden jar.—Any two conducting substances kept apart by glass will answer just as well, or indeed very much better than the water and the hand. Tinfoil is pasted over the surfaces of a glass jar, both inside and outside, to within a few inches of the top, and then the jar is covered with a cover made of hard wood, through which passes a brass rod. There is a ball on the top of this rod, and a chain at its lower end that reaches down to the bottom of the jar.

How may the jar be charged?—Let the jar be held in the hand with its knob very near to the conductor of the machine. Sparks of electricity will fly into the knob; in a dark room they look like little flashes of lightning. After a while, when the sparks are feeble, the jar is said to be *charged*.

How may it be discharged?—Should a person accidentally touch the knob of the charged jar with one hand

and the outside tinfoil with the other, he would feel a shock which would startle and perhaps injure him. His body is a good conductor, and the shock is due to the discharge of the jar through it. A discharge will always occur when any conductor reaches from the knob to the outside coating of the jar. A bent wire with a glass handle is generally used for the purpose.

ELECTRICITY BY CHEMICAL ACTION.

What is meant by chemical action?—When a piece of paper burns it ceases to be paper, as every one knows, and changes into smoke and ashes. The *nature* of the substance is changed during the action. Now this shows what we mean by chemical action. It is an action by which the *nature of a substance is changed.*

We will mention another case. Put some bits of zinc into a goblet and pour upon them some weak sulphuric acid. The fluid will soon begin to boil violently, and bubbles of gas will be given off, so that often, if a lighted match is held near, the gas will take fire. This will give the curious appearance of *water on fire.* After a while the action will stop, but not until much and perhaps all the zinc has been used up.

Why is this action a chemical action?—In this case both the zinc and the acid are changed into other substances, and on this account the action is called a chemical action.

Will it produce electricity?—Now let a strip of zinc and another of copper be placed side by side in a glass vessel nearly full of weak sulphuric acid, but do not let them touch each other. Have a wire fastened to the upper end of each metal. It will be found that whenever th se wires come together electricity will act through them. This electricity is due to the chemical action going on in the vessel.

What is this apparatus called?—This simple apparatus is called a *Voltaic circuit.* The electricity it gives is often called *Galvanism* and often *Voltaic electricity.* These names were given in honor of Galvani, who first studied this force, and of Volta, who also made it a study, and found out many new things about it.

What are the poles of the circuit?—The ends of the wires are commonly called the poles, of the circuit. One is called the *positive* pole and the other is called the *negative* pole.

When the poles are in contact, or when there is any conductor which joins them together, the circuit is said to be *closed*, but when they are separated the circuit is said to be *open.*

What effects can this circuit produce?—The electric force in this simple circuit is very weak. It can make its presence known by a feeble spark seen in the dark at the moment when the wires are separated, but which can be seldom seen at all in daylight. It also causes bubbles of gas to rise alongside of the copper plate when the circuit is closed. And, what is more curious still is that it will turn a magnetic needle, when the wires are laid lengthwise of the needle, *without touching it.* You will learn more of these effects at some future time.

Can greater effects be obtained?—Very much greater effects can be obtained by using a different apparatus. One of the best kinds is the *Bunsen's battery.*

The picture Fig. 85 will help us to understand how the Bunsen's battery is arranged. It consists of—

1. A glass or earthenware vessel, containing
2. Dilute sulphuric acid. In this stands

3. A hollow cylinder of zinc.   Inside of this is
4. A porous earthen cup, filled with
5. Strong nitric acid.   And finally in this
6. A rod or block of carbon is immersed.

Fig. 65.

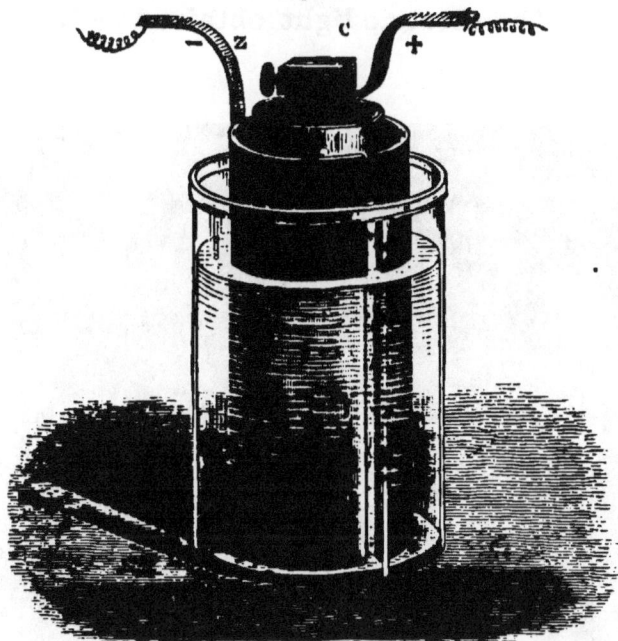

One wire or metallic bar goes from the carbon; this is
the positive pole: another goes from the zinc, and this is
the negative pole.

**How may the power of the battery be increas-
ed?**—By joining several of these single batteries together
electricity of almost any power may be obtained.

The zinc of each cell may be joined to the carbon of
the next.   The first carbon is the positive pole, and the
last zinc is the negative pole.   When these poles are
joined together a powerful electric force is obtained, by
which most wonderful effects are caused.

Describe the electric heat.—If a fine iron wire is stretched between the poles of a strong battery it will be quickly heated white hot, and actually burned up, even when several inches long. Copper, zinc, and other metals melt readily and are burned by electricity.

How is the electric light obtained?—In the pic-

Fig. 86.

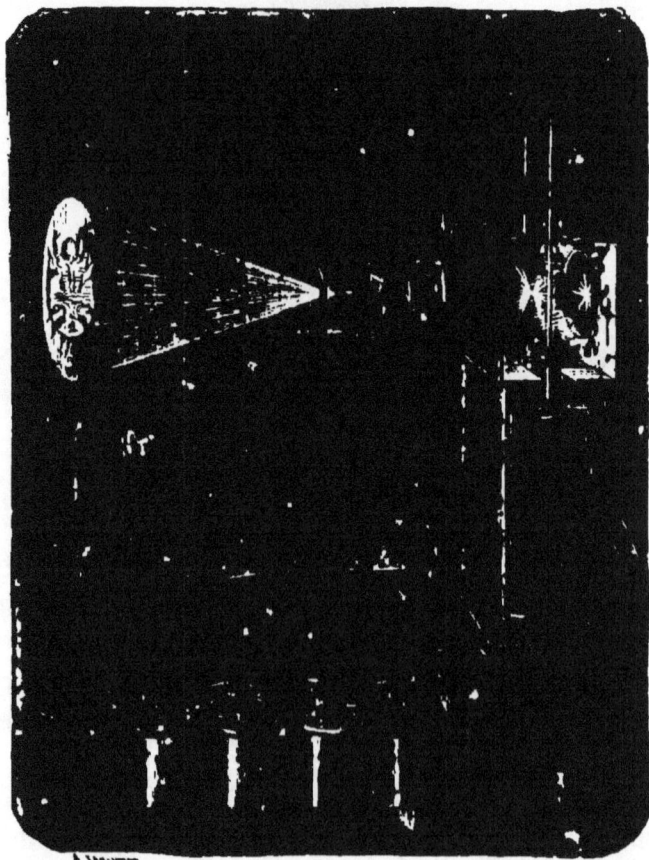

ture, Fig. 86, the electric light is represented as in use. The battery, a very strong one of 50 or perhaps 100 cells, stands upon the floor. The lamp stands upon the table. The light is obtained by having the poles tipped with charcoal and then drawing them a little way apart. It is of the most dazzling brightness. The light is not due to the *burning* of the charcoal, for it is as bright when made in a vacuum where the carbon cannot burn at all.

In the picture this light is being used in a microscope. It is made to pass through an insect and afterwards through convex lenses, which form a magnified image of the creature upon the screen.

"With this instrument it is possible to show the smallest objects magnified almost indefinitely. A human hair will appear as large as a broomstick; an ordinary flea will look the size of a sheep, and the smallest animalcules will be visible in all their beauty of form and color as clearly as if they were seen with the naked eye."

The electric light has been used also, sometimes, to enable workmen to labor at night. When it is necessary to accomplish a great work speedily, it may go on without stopping, the sun giving the workmen light by day and the electric light by night. See Fig. 87.

How may water be decomposed?—We need only put the poles of a strong battery into water and bubbles of gas will rapidly rise from both. The water is changed into *two gases*.

The picture, Fig. 88, will show us how the experiment is usually made.

We see that the wires from a battery go up into a vessel of water and that two tall tubes are placed over them. These tubes are there to catch the little bubbles of gas into which the water is changed. They were filled with water at the beginning of the experiment, but as the

Fig. 87.

bubbles rise they drive the water out.   One tube is filling twice as fast as the other, you may notice.

Fig. 88.

What gases are these ?—One of these gases is *hydrogen*. the other is *oxygen*.   The hydrogen is given off most rapidly.

The electricity in this case helps us to learn that water is made up of two very light and colorless gases, hydrogen and oxygen, and that it contains twice as much of the first as of the second.

A great many other substances may be decomposed by electricity.

ELECTRO-MAGNETISM.

What apparatus needed to show the effect of electricity upon iron?—Take a long piece of covered copper wire and wind it many times around a rod of soft iron. Fix one end of this wire to one pole of the battery and the other end to the other pole. The electricity will then act around the iron rod and we can study its effects.

What effect is produced?—Open the circuit by taking the wire away from one pole of the battery, and we may by trial find that the iron has no especial attraction for small bits of iron which are brought in contact with it; but close the circuit, and instantly the bits of iron will cling to the rod and be held by it as long as the electricity acts.

This experiment shows that electricity makes a bar of iron magnetic by acting around it.

What are such magnets called?—Such magnets are called *electro-magnets* because their magnetism is caused by electricity.

In what form are they usually made?—These electro-magnets are generally made in the shape of the horse-shoe magnet, and the wire is wound a great many times around each branch.

In the picture (Fig. 89) we see one of the electro-magnets fastened in a frame.

This picture also shows the result of a curious experiment. A box of nails is shown ·below. This box was lifted until the magnet touched the nails and then was

Fig. 89.

slowly let down again. The magnet lifted all the nails it touched: these nails lifted others, and others then clung to them until, as you see in the picture, a chain of nails hung from the ends of the magnet and rested upon the box below.

How long will the iron stay magnetic?—Just at the moment the electric circuit is opened the nails will drop, every one into the box. The iron will be a magnet only while the electricity is acting aronnd it.

What instrument acts on this principle?—The

electric telegraph acts upon this principle. In one city there is a " key " by which a person may open and close an electric circuit as often as he pleases. The wires of this circuit reach over the country to a distant city an l are there joined to the coils of an electro-magnet. Just above the poles of this magnet is an armature kept a little way from them by a spring.

Now let a person press the key with his finger and close the circuit : the electricity will dart through the wires to the distant city and around the electro-magnet, and the magnet will pull the armature down. When he lifts his finger the electricity will not act; the magnet ceases to be magnetic and the armature is lifted by the spring. Just as often as he presses the key the armature will be drawn down.

The next thing to know in order to understand this wonderful instrument, is that there is a steel point fastened to the armature, so that every time the armature is drawn to the magnet, the point is pulled against a strip of paper and makes a mark upon it. A person in one city can thus be making marks upon paper in another city many miles away.

The marks consist of dots and straight lines, and each letter of the alphabet is represented by some arrangement of these marks. For instance, a dot followed by a dash, thus : - —, means A ; and a dash followed by a dot, thus, — - stands for N ; while a dash and two dots — - - stands for D. You see, then, how the man at the key may write the word AND by making these dots and dashes. It would look like this, - — — - — - -, and one who knows the alphabet by dots and dashes can read these characters even when a thousand miles away from the place from which the message is sent.

This description is only an outline of the plan of the electric telegraph. Every boy and girl should seek a chance to *see* the instrument itself, for from it can be learned, better than from any book, just how the messages are sent and taken.

MACHINERY.

What is shown in Fig. 90?—In Fig. 90 we see the picture of a man trying to move a block of stone. It is much too heavy for him to lift, and you notice that he has taken a long bar to assist him. Putting one end of it under the stone, and resting the bar upon a block C, he pushes down upon the other end, and in this way lifts the stone.

Fig. 90.

Explain the action more fully.—We see that the bar rests upon the prop C, and that the end B cannot be pushed down without moving the other end A, up. Now when the part C B is so much longer than the part C A, the man by his own weight can lift a stone very much heavier than he himself is.

What is this bar called?—This bar is called a *lever*. This name is given to any bar that can be used in this manner. A *lever* is an inflexible bar which can turn freely upon a pivot or prop.

Define Power, Weight, and Fulcrum.—The strength which the man exerts at B is called the *power;* we speak

of the stone to be moved as the *weight*, and call the prop
C the *fulcrum*.

Levers are not always moved by hand, nor are they
always used to move stones, and yet these same terms are
used. The *power* is any force by which the lever is to be
moved. The *weight* is any resistance which is to be overcome. The *fulcrum* is the support on which the lever
moves.

What does Fig. 91 A show?—In Fig. 91 A, the lever
is shown without the laborer and the stone. P represents
the place of the power; W represents the place of the
weight, and F the fulcrum. The fulcrum is in this case
between the power and the weight.

Fig. 91.

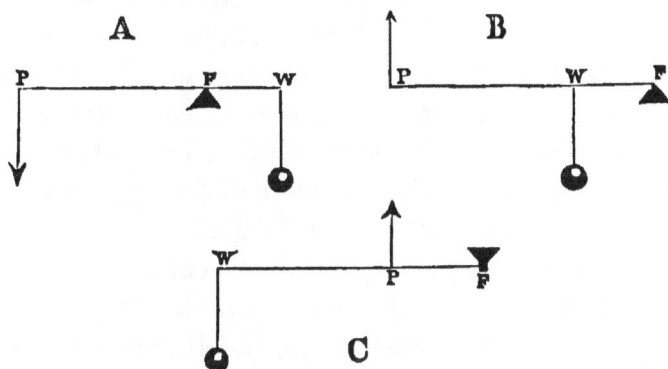

Is this always the case?—But this is not always the
order of arrangement. In Fig. 91 B, the weight W is between the fulcrum F and the power P. The weight being
near the fulcrum, is lifted by raising the more distant end
of the lever.

In Fig. 91 C, the power is between the fulcrum and the
weight. Here also the power must pull upward to lift the
weight. Now these three figures represent levers of the
three classes.

Describe the three classes of lever.—In a lever of
8*

the *first class* the fulcrum is between the power and the weight (Fig. 91 A). In a lever of the *second class* the weight is between the power and the fulcrum (Fig. 91 B). In a lever of the *third class* the power is between the fulcrum and the weight (Fig. 91 C).

All levers, of whatever form or use, belong to these three classes.

Mention some levers of the first class.—The handle of a common pump is a lever of the first class: the piston and the water are the weight, the hand of whomsoever does the work is the power, while the pivot on which the handle turns is the fulcrum.

The balance of a tradesman is another example: the body to be weighed, put into one scale-pan, is the weight; the weights put into the other pan are the power; while the pivot on which the beam turns is the fulcrum.

Examples of the second class.—The handles of a wheelbarrow are levers of the second class: the axle of the wheel is the fulcrum on which they turn when lifted; whatever is placed in the barrow is the weight, while the hand of the laborer is the power to lift it.

An oar is another example. The boat is the weight to be moved; the hand of the boatman is the power to move it; while the water against which the other end of the oar presses is the fulcrum.

Example of the third class.—When a ladder is raised by resting one end on the ground and lifting upon a round somewhat farther up, it is a lever of the third class. The end on the ground is the fulcrum; the hand of the man is the power; while the weight of the ladder, most of which is beyond the hand, is the weight.

What relation exists between power and weight? —In Fig. 90, if the distance from A, the place where the weight rests on the lever, to C, the fulcrum, is one-fourth the distance from C to B, then the weight may be balanced by a power only one-fourth as great. The power will be just as many times *less* than the weight as the distance from it to the fulcrum is times *greater* than the distance from the weight to the fulcrum. If the distance of the power from the fulcrum is *ten* times as far as the distance from the weight to the fulcrum, then the weight will be balanced by a power only *one-tenth* as great as itself.

State the law.—This principle, briefly stated, is as follows: "The power and weight will *balance each other* when they are to each other *inversely* as their distances from the fulcrum."

This principle is called the law of equilibrium for the lever. It holds good in all the three classes.

To *move* the weight, the power must be a little greater than this principle would make it.

What is a compound lever?—When two or more levers are made to act one upon another in succession, so that a power applied to the first lifts a weight applied to the last, the instrument is called a *compound lever*.

What does Fig. 92 show?—Fig. 92 shows how a weight may be lifted by fastening one end of a rope to it

Fig. 92.

and winding the rope up on a cylinder. In this way water is often raised from deep wells. By turning the crank the upper part of the rope is wound upon the cylinder, and the bucket, hooked upon the lower end, is raised.

What often takes the place of the crank?—Instead of a crank B, to turn the cylinder, a wheel C is very often used. The power is applied to the circumference of the wheel, sometimes by means of a rope, sometimes by means of a band, sometimes by means of cogs, and in various other ways.

What are such machines called?—A machine such as represented in Fig. 92 is called a "*Wheel and axle.*" The cylinder upon which the rope winds is the "*axle,*" while the "*wheel*" may be an actual wheel or a crank, both of which are shown in the picture, or it may have other forms still. Whatever shape this part may have the machine is called the "wheel and axle."

What is the relation between the power and the weight?—When the weight is just as many times greater than the power as the radius of the wheel is greater than the radius of the axle, the two forces will just balance. In other words: "The power and weight will balance, when the power is to the weight as the radius of the axle is to the radius of the wheel."

This principle is called the law of equilibrium for the wheel and axle. To *move* the weight, the power must be made greater than this law requires.

How are wheels and axles often combined?—Many wheels and axles are sometimes turned by a single power. In this case motion is communicated from wheel to axle or from axle to wheel by means of bands or cogs. If by a power on one wheel its axle is turned, and a band passes around this axle and a second wheel, the second axle will be turned also. Great power may in this way be obtained.

How may rapid motion be secured?—If the power be applied to the circumference of the axle instead of the wheel, and if a band pass around the wheel and a second axle, the second wheel will be put into very rapid motion.

What is shown in Fig. 93?— In this figure we can see how a heavy weight may be lifted by fastening it to the end of a rope which passes up over a grooved wheel, and then pulling downward upon the other end.

Fig. 93.

What is such a grooved wheel called?—A grooved wheel used for such a purpose is called a *pulley;* and in this case, since it is firmly fastened in a fixed support, it is called a *fixed pulley.*

What advantage in its use?—The only advantage gained by means of the fixed pulley consists in being able to change the direction in which the power acts. A man, for example, can exert his strength to better advantage *pulling downward* than *lifting upward,* and if a load is to be lifted the fixed pulley allows him to use his power in this better way. He gains in no other way; if the load weighs 100 lbs., he must pull with a force equal to 100 lbs., and indeed a little more, since the rope and pulley take up some of his strength to move them.

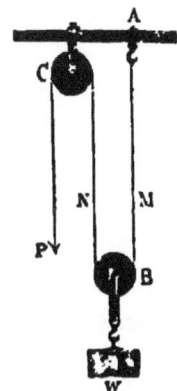

Fig. 94.

What is a movable pulley?—The case is very different when the pulley is arranged as in Fig. 94. In this arrangement the weight is hung from the axis of the pulley, B, and is to be lifted by means of the rope which is fastened to the beam at A, and then after passing under the pulley B, goes over the fixed pulley C. By pulling upon the rope at P, the pulley B will be lifted and will carry the weight up with it. A pulley which moves with the weight is called a *movable pulley*.

What advantage is gained ?—Now it is easy to see that the weight is held up by the two branches of rope, *m* and *n*, and that each branch holds one-half of it. But the half which rests on *m* is sustained by the beam, leaving only the other half, which rests on *n*, to be lifted by the power at P.

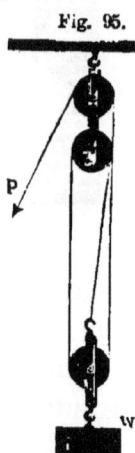

Fig. 95.

When, with a movable pulley, there are *two* branches of rope to sustain the weight, the power may be only *one-half* the weight.

In Fig. 95 there are *three* branches of the rope which hold the weight and share it equally between them. In this case the power need be only *one-third* as great as the weight to balance it.

What general principle does this illustrate ?—In all cases the power needed to balance any weight will be found by dividing that weight by the *number of branches* of the rope which supports it.

Will this law apply in all cases ?—In the cases considered you will notice that there is a *single rope* winding around all the pulleys. Now the law holds good whenever the weight is supported in this way, provided the branches of the rope are parallel. There are a great many other ways of arranging the pulleys, not as common as this, however, and in such cases the law stated above does not hold good.

Mention some purposes for which pulleys are used.—Pulleys are often used for lifting heavy articles of merchandise to the upper stories of warehouses. They may be seen also where buildings of stone are being erected, and heavy blocks are to be raised to considerable height. But more numerous than anywhere else, you will

find pulleys on shipboard, where they are used by the
seamen in managing the rigging of the ship.

What is an inclined plane ?—When a drayman wishes
to lift a cask of sugar from the sidewalk to his dray he
does not lay hold of it and raise it vertically, as he might
do with a lesser weight, but he accomplishes the work
far more easily by rolling it up along a plank reaching
obliquely from the ground to the dray. The *inclined
surface* of the plank is called an *inclined plane.* Any
inclined surface over which weights are to be moved is
an inclined plane.

**What is meant by the terms length and height of
the plane ?**—In Fig. 96 a weight W is shown resting on
an inclined surface A B, balanced by a smaller weight P.
Now the distance A B is called the *length* of the inclined
plane, and the vertical distance C B is called the *height* of
the plane.

Fig. 96.

In the plane used by the drayman the length of the
plank from the sidewalk to the dray is the length of the
inclined plane, while the height of the dray above the
walk is the height of the plane.

What relation exists between power and weight ?
—If the weight W is 100 lbs. and the *height* of the plane
is one half the *length*, then the power to balance the
weight need be only one-half the weight, or 50 lbs.

If the height is $\frac{1}{10}$ of the length of the plane, the power
need be only $\frac{1}{10}$ the weight.

The general principle or *law* is this; the power and

weight will balance when the power is to the weight as the height of the plane is to its length.

Under what conditions will this law hold good ?—This law holds good only when the power is exerted in a direction *parallel to the length* of the plane; in any other direction the relation is different. Moreover, friction of the weight upon the plane has much to do with the relation of power to weight. The law would be quite true only when friction did not exist, a case which never occurs in practice. If the weight is to be balanced on the plane, then friction helps the power to do it; but if the weight is to be moved up the plane, friction is a hindrance instead of a help.

Explain Fig. 97.—This picture, Fig. 97, shows how barrels are drawn up from or let down into a cellar. It is a case of the inclined plane which you can easily understand and explain without further help.

Fig. 97.

How does a woodman sometimes split his blocks ? —When blocks of wood are to be split, a smaller block of wood or metal, made thick at one end and tapering to an edge at the other, is driven into the end of it, as shown in Fig. 98. The tapering block is called a *wedge*.

Fig. 98.

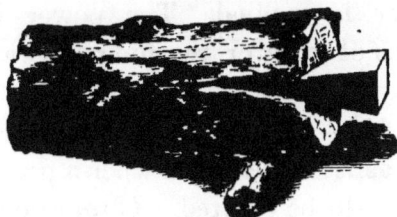

What are the power and weight in this case ?— The energy of the woodman's blows upon the back of the wedge is the *power ;* the cohesion of the wood is the *weight*, and it is not easy to find the relation between these two forces. Hence we cannot here state any *law* according to which the ratio of power and weight, when they balance each other, can be found.

What familiar instruments act on the principle of the wedge ?—The chisel of the carpenter is a wedge; so is the blade of a pocket-knife; each having a sharp edge, and being thicker at a distance from it. The chisel is usually driven by blows; the knife urged by pressure; but the cohesion of the wood is the resistance, or the *weight* to be overcome by both. All cutting and piercing instruments are different forms of the wedge.

Describe the screw.—The screw consists of a cylinder having a spiral groove cut around its circumference. The small screw used by carpenters for joining the parts of their work, on a small scale illustrates this arrangement. When the screw is to be used as a machine, the cylinder is made larger, sometimes a few inches, sometimes several inches in diameter. The projecting edges left between the parts of the spiral groove are called *threads*, and the screw works through an opening in a firm block having a spiral groove cut upon its interior surface into which these threads just fit. This block is called the *nut*, or sometimes the *concave screw*.

The top of the screw is called its *head :* it is the part to which the power is applied. The power is generally applied by means of a lever reaching outward from the head.

Explain Fig. 99.—This cut represents a screw set in a firm framework, as it is often used when a great pressure is to be exerted. C represents the head of the screw, and B the lever by which it can be turned. The block N through which the screw works is the nut.

Fig. 99.

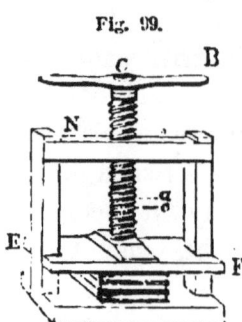

When the screw is turned by the lever it advances through the nut and pushes the movable block E F down upon the body to be pressed. An enormous pressure may, in this way, be exerted upon this body.

The *power* is applied at B, and the pressure exerted is the *weight*.

What is the relation between the power and weight?—As the screw is turned the power at B must travel around a large circle, and when it has gone once around, the screw will have advanced through the nut a distance *a c*, the distance between two contiguous parts of the thread. Now it is found that the weight will be as many times greater than the power, as the circumference through which the power travels is times greater than this little distance *a c*. In other words, the law may be stated: " The power and weight will balance, when the power is to the weight as the distance between two contiguous threads is to the circumference in which the power moves."

How many machines have now been described ?—We have now described *six simple machines* by which weights may be lifted or resistance overcome. Let us bring their names together.

The Lever.	The Inclined plane.
" Wheel and axle.	" Wedge.
" Pulley.	" Screw.

There are no others. All forms of machinery are made by combining these six. Just as when you learned the twenty-six letters of the alphabet you possessed all the characters used in the many thousands of words of our language, so, having learned of these six simple machines, you have learned of all the elements out of which ingenious men have contrived the wonderful variety of machinery to be found among civilized nations.

What one principle holds good in the action of all these machines?—A *small power* acting *swiftly* may put a *large weight* in *slow motion;* or a *great power* acting *slowly* may put a *small weight* in *rapid motion.*

This law holds good in all forms of machinery, what is lacking in *force* must be made up in *velocity.* And in just this lies the advantage of using machinery. It helps man to transform *velocity* into *power* to overcome resistance. No power can be created by it, and wherever power is gained it is *bought* and *paid for* in *velocity.*

By what agents is power to move machinery exerted?—Animals, water, wind, and stéam are the agents or powers most commonly applied to move machinery. Men or horses, by means of pulleys or wheels, may be seen lifting stones where large buildings are being erected. Saw-mills and flouring-mills are often worked by " water power" acting upon the circumference of large wheels. Wind-mills for pumping water and for other purposes are turned by the wind, while in the steam-engine and all the vast machinery in the arts moved by it, the motive power is steam.

What is meant by the term "Horse-Power"?—The term *horse-power* is used in estimating the effect which a steam-engine or other machine can produce. The term *has no reference to the animal whose name is used:* it simply means a certain amount of work. A power to lift 33,000 lbs. through 1 foot in 1 minute is a "horse-power." So when an engine is described as an engine of "10 horse-power," we understand that it is able to do a work equal to that of lifting 10 times 33,000 lbs. 1 foot in 1 minute.

THE STEAM-ENGINE.

How can steam be applied to machinery?—The expansive power of steam (p. 142) was known long before any means were devised to use it in machinery. Animals could be harnessed to a machine easily: water and wind would act upon wheels and turn them, but how could *steam* be harnessed or applied? In the open air steam is as feeble as an insect, but when confined in a close vessel its efforts to expand produce enormous pressures. If it can be *confined* and yet be properly brought against a machine, the machine will be put in motion. This is accomplished in the *steam-engine*.

How is this accomplished?—For this purpose a cylinder is provided, having a piston fitting its interior nicely, and able to move smoothly from one end to the other back and forth. Steam is made to enter the cylinder first at one end of the cylinder, then at the other, and the pressure of the steam behind the piston knocks it back and forth from end to end with enormous force.

Explain Fig. 100.—Fig. 100 will illustrate this brief description. C represents the cylinder, and P the piston which can move freely from end to end. S represents the pipe through which the steam comes from the boiler. It enters the box shown by the open space, *y*, and the steam passes from there in a direction shown by the upper arrow, and enters the cylinder at the top. Once in the cylinder it expands against the piston and pushes it down, the old and useless steam below, passing at the same time through an opening at the bottom, and thence up to the space O, and away through a pipe not shown in the cut.

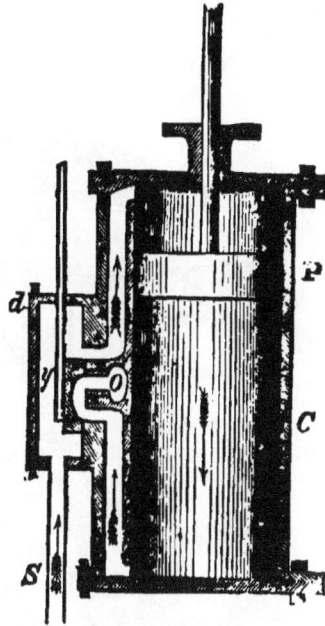

When the piston has almost reached the bottom of the cylinder, the block *y slides up*, and covers the passage leading to the top, but uncovers the one leading to the bottom. The steam is then forced through the lower passage to the bottom of the cylinder, and, expanding there, drives the piston to the top again.

The block *y* then slides down and opens the upper passage: the steam goes to the top behind the piston and drives it down. The block *y* then slides up again and opens the lower passage: the steam goes to the bottom behind the piston, and drives it to the top.

Fig. 100.

You see that by the *slide valve, y,* the steam goes first to one end of the cylinder, then to the other, and thus drives the piston P back and forth.

Now this piston P has a rod firmly fastened to it which reaches up through the top of the cylinder, and which is pushed out and drawn in by the moving piston. It is called the "piston-rod." The *outer end of this piston-rod acts as a power* to move levers or turn cranks, and thus give motion to machinery.

The steam moves the piston, the piston moves the piston-rod, and the piston-rod gives motion to the machinery outside.

Explain Fig. 101.—The picture, Fig. 101, shows how the piston-rod gives motion to machinery in one form of the steam-engine.

Fig. 101.

In the first place, at the left, we see the cylinder with one side cut away, so that we may see the piston (P) inside. The steam is supposed to be entering the valve-box at S and going to the upper part of the cylinder, pushing the piston down, just as we described when we explained Fig. 100.

The piston-rod A D is fastened to one end of the large and strong lever II K. As the piston goes down it pulls this end of the lever down and throws the other end K, up. When the piston rises in the cylinder the piston-rod pushes the lever end II, up, and throws the other end K, down.

Now as the lever at K goes up and down, it pulls and pushes upon the strong arm J, and in this way turns the crank C. The large wheel W W, fixed upon the axle, will thus be put in motion.

Where may we find engines of this form?—This form of engine is often used on steamboats. The great lever H K may be seen above decks moving alternately up and down when the steamer is in motion. It is sometimes called the " walking-beam." The strong arm J reaches down into the boat and turns an enormous iron axle, which reaches quite through the boat from side to side, and has a *paddle-wheel* at each end.

Is motion always communicated in this way?— The way in which the piston-rod gives motion to other parts is very different in different engines. There is no " walking-beam " in a *locomotive*, you know. You can see in Fig. 101 that the piston-rod is jointed at B. Now in the locomotive engine the outer end of the jointed part D is fastened directly to the *" drive-wheel "* of the locomotive at a point between its centre and its circumference. The cylinder lies horizontal, and as the rod A moves back and forth the " drive-wheel " is turned and the locomotive rolled forward.

Engines used for other purposes than those just mentioned are made in different forms. A visit to some manufactory, where you may see for yourself the construction and action of one of these most wonderful machines, will do more to make you acquainted with its parts and their uses than can be gained from books, even though you study long and faithfully.

What is a high-pressure engine?—Sometimes the steam, after pushing the piston, is made to escape into the air in puffs. This is done in the locomotive engine, and it gives rise to the irregular puffs heard especially when the engine starts. Now this steam must be *pushed* out *against* *the air*, which presses with a force of 15 lbs. to the square inch to keep it in the cylinder. The steam which moves the piston must exert force enough to overcome this pressure before it can exert any to move the machinery outside. Its pressure must be at least 15 lbs. to the square inch *higher* than the machinery would otherwise require. On this account the engine is called a *high-pressure* engine.

What is a low-pressure engine?—In other engines the steam, after having moved the piston, is allowed to pass through a pipe into a closed chamber, where, by cold water, it is condensed. The withdrawal and condensation of the steam removes the pressure from in front of the piston, and the force of the steam behind it may be all expended in moving the machinery. Since the steam has less work to do, it can do it with less pressure than in the high-pressure engine, and this form is on this account called the *low-pressure* engine.

www.ingramcontent.com/pod-product-compliance
Lightning Source LLC
Chambersburg PA
CBHW030842270326
41928CB00007B/1173